We Don't Talk About It.
Ever.

We Don't Talk About It.
Ever.

*A girl who searched for love but found
destruction instead*

Desiree-Anne Martin

For Isabella Rachael and Scarlett Grace,
my heart, my hope, my truth.

First published by MFBooks Joburg, an imprint of Jacana Media
(Pty) Ltd, in 2018

© Desiree-Anne Martin, 2018
Author photograph © Samantha Squire-Howe
Anaïs Nin quote from *The Early Diaries Of Anaïs Nin: 1927–1931*, Volume IV.
© Rupert Pole, 1985. Reprinted by permission of Houghton Mifflin Harcourt
Publishing Company. All rights reserved.

©Desiree-Anne Martin, 2020
Second edition published by Seven & Eight Integrated Consulting
Wynberg Cape Town 7800
South Africa
www.desireeannemartin.com

ISBN 978-1-990944-62-8

Cover design by Anastasya Eliseeva
Editing by Sean Fraser Proofreading
by Linda Da Nova
Set in Sabon 11/15p

"I take pleasure in my transformations. I look quiet and consistent, but few know how many women there are in me."

– ANAÏS NIN

Contents

Part 3: Fuck the Rules

Part 4: The New Rules

Part 5: Bending the Rules

Prologue

Words are my drug of choice.

They are my refuge, my panacea. They are the antidote to the poison that runs through every artery and vein of the anatomy of my childhood. Long before the hastily inhaled cigarettes that burned my throat during second break, half-hiding in between the crumbling headstones of the long-forgotten brides of Jesus up at the small convent cemetery. Long before the bottles of Bioplus mixed in cups of too-strong coffee that kept my heavy eyelids from drooping while I poured over mind-numbing high school calculus equations and brain-crushing historical facts about dead people and disremembered places. Long before the back end of the toothbrush connected with my epiglottis, forcing the acidic, bilious contents of my stomach to lurch out of my mouth, leaving telltale splatters across the toilet bowl. Long before the shiny blister packs of slimming tablets that would make my heart race and jaw tremble, inspiring me to rub my hungry, concave belly with reticent glee. Long before that first sip of cheap red wine seeped its way into my parched veins and quenched my thirsty cells until it felt like I had come home at last. Long before I submerged myself in the unbearable heat of that scorching bathwater over and over again to relieve the intolerable pain of what lay trapped within. Long before the codeine daydreams and the benzo comas.

Long before the endless stream of men and women who filled my mouth, my cunt, filling any void that existed there. Long before LSD made my unconscious bleed all over my reality. Long before the dizzying nights of delirious dancing spurred on by the lines of cocaine I snorted up my raw nostrils. Long before the chemical hazy halcyon Ecstasy-laced weekends where I fell in love with everything and everyone except myself. And even before the crack pipe burned my bottom lip and pinned me up against the wall, scrambling for an exit route; and yes, even before the needle pricked my flesh and sent that noxious, precious elixir straight to my orphaned soul and cradled it and made it whole. Long before all of that ... there were words.

I remember smuggling a book into the toilet during my designated nap time on a Sunday afternoon when I was four years old. Even then I had problems sleeping when I was supposed to. I was teaching myself to read, having stolen my older brother's *Kathy and Mark* reader from his brown, boxy school case. Kathy wore a bright red dress, milky white skin framed by hair cut in a severe brown bob that never moved no matter how much she was urged by Mark to "Run, Kathy, run!" Mark also ran a lot, in his blue shorts and knee-high socks, accompanied everywhere by their dog, Spot. They ran everywhere, they frequently sat on the mat, they rode on the bus to the city with their mum, who wore a smart green hat and a coat, and once they drove in the car with their dad who also wore a hat, which he took off every evening when he came home from work.

I recall sitting on that cold tiled toilet floor, the avocado green and white-patterned tiles, tracing the words with my index finger and matching them to the garishly coloured illustrations of a smug dawdling tortoise and an arrogant reckless hare. I remember my frustration at not being able to decipher some of the words. I wanted to know them. I needed to know *what happened*. I remember the look on my mother's face as it appeared at the crack of the open door: her surprise, then anger and disappointment. I felt ashamed, found out. I instinctively hid my book behind my back. I hid my words. Like I would hide everything that would come after.

And later I would achieve small literary victories: having stared for what seemed like an eternity at the large, ornately framed black-and-white photograph of my mother on her wedding day that rested on the cream melamine TV unit, trying to make sense of the words printed beneath the photo. Then one day the phonetically pieced together "VAN KALKER P-A-H-O-T-A-G-R-A-P-E-E-H-Y-A-H" suddenly and magically made sense and I yelled at the top of my childish voice, much as I imagine Archimedes proclaimed, "Eureka!"

"PHOTOGRAPHY!"

I marched triumphantly around the house repeating the newly discovered word over and over again, "Photography! Photography! *Photography!*" This made no sense to any of my family but I didn't care to explain it. The word, that unearthed treasure, that reconstructed jewel, was *mine*.

And when my brother was in Standard 1 and I in Sub A, he would climb into the car after school bemoaning the fact that he had to learn a four-stanza poem about seashells on the sandy seashore by the end of that week. I had it memorised and could recite it by the end of the 20-minute drive home.

Once I could read, I consumed books – in fact, all the reading matter I could lay my hands on. I inhaled words, chewing and digesting them greedily at any given opportunity. Blurry-eyed and bent over my runny porridge, during car rides despite my stomach swirling and my head pounding from carsickness, propped up in my bed long after the 8 o'clock TV news jingle had signalled it was bedtime, during school holidays when I would scour prescribed setwork books and finish them long before the academic year even began. Anywhere and everywhere, I wrapped words around me like a steely suit of armour.

I would write too. Inspired by *The Secret Diary of Adrian Mole*, I started my first 'Secret Diary' at age nine. I would religiously scribble my childish observations and fickle feelings down on paper in my untidy, oft-criticised script. I would use the diaries as a tool of self-expression but also as a tool of blatant manipulation, leaving them open on certain pages in strategically placed locales for my prying mother to find if I wanted to communicate something that I was too afraid to do directly. Like 'asking' for my first bra.

I found solace in the fantastical worlds of books. Words became my escape, my safe haven from the lies and the secrets, from the trauma and the terror.

Later I found refuge in the words of scripts and dense screenplays. Words that had a transformative effect on my domain, and even more so on my very identity. In drama class at school, at the theatre school that I secretly auditioned for and gained acceptance into when I was just 13 years old, words would morph me into anything, anyone. As long as it wasn't me. I could escape my reality and slip into another space and time just by uttering a few lines or manipulating my larynx and changing my accent. I hid behind the safety of others' words because mine always seemed insufficient or often entirely absent.

Words held unimaginable power. Words, when pieced together in a certain manner, exerted great influence. I became adept at weaving stories, a mixture of fabrications and quasi-truths, to cover up the reality of how utterly ruined I felt inside. I learned early on that I was a remarkably convincing liar and that deception slipped from my forked tongue with ease, without reason or provocation. I lived in a constant state of semi-realism, blending fantasy with reality and spinning it around myself like a comforting cocoon. I used anything, any form of control, to not feel the excruciating pain of the truth.

But I am done with deceit. Lies no longer hold any allure for me. Now I seek true words that will, somehow, begin to heal that which has been broken.

PART 1

The Rules

CHAPTER 1

The Mistake

I was a mistake.

While my brother's arrival – though almost two months premature, in the late, sticky summer of 1974 – was perfectly planned and celebrated, mine came unexpectedly. My brother was born on 17 February 1974 on my parents' second wedding anniversary and he would always share that special day alongside them, for better or for worse. My mother had a thing for unusual double-barrelled names. My bonny, though minuscule brother was thus named Alcid-John, a hybrid of my father's name: Alfred John and my father's close friend Sidney. It was an unusual name even for the seventies and even more so later in his life, when he'd have to endure crinkle-eyed confusion, mild teasing and general self-loathing.

After my brother's birth, my mother was duly informed that she could no longer conceive, which, at the age of 36, she accepted. One child, she felt, completed their little family and would be more than sufficient. So when my Ma Eileen suggested my mother should go to the gynaecologist and take a pregnancy test when she started complaining of minor bodily ailments, she scoffed at the idea, but quickly complied because one very rarely argued with Ma Eileen.

As my mother sat in the cool, tiled hallway outside the doctor's rooms, waiting for the results of both the urine test and the physical exam she had just undergone, chain smoking her long, thin, white cigarettes, she was surprised by two things: firstly, the kind, elderly doctor deftly swatting the lit cigarette out of her mouth as he approached and, secondly, the news that she was, in fact, already five months' pregnant.

She had displayed no outward signs of pregnancy or symptoms common for one so far along. Years later, when I was to fall carelessly pregnant at the age of 18 – my breasts painfully tender, clutching the toilet bowl and violently ill both with confusion and morning sickness at a mere eight weeks along – I would wonder at how very out of touch my mother must have been with her body that she had managed to reach five months without recognising my growing presence within her. My mother and father would have a mere two months to get used to the idea of me.

She was working as a bookkeeper at NU-Pharmacy, a chemist in Claremont, when her waters broke abruptly and prematurely all over her office floor. True to her almost obsessive-compulsive nature, my mother fetched a mop and bucket from the storeroom and cleaned up her own amniotic mess before making arrangements to head to Somerset Hospital in Green Point. No amount of spinning of the rotary-dial telephone could connect her to my father so he was noticeably absent at my birth. I was born two hours later without much complication.

When my father did finally hear the news of my arrival, he plonked my toddler brother into the passenger seat and drove from suburb to suburb, relative to friend, both of them melodiously announcing, "We have a sister! We have a sister!" My father got hopelessly inebriated on celebratory drinks offered by all they called on their journey.

In keeping with her trend of foisting unusual names on her children, my mother told the doctor that I was to be called Dezanne, named after my Uncle Desmond and cemented to the name Anne, which she thought was "rather pretty". The doctor either misunderstood or thought that no child should be burdened with such a title so wrote "Desiree-Anne" on the birth certificate, inadvertently throwing in a hyphen.

I was ridiculously small – "You could fit in a shoebox" – so was immediately incubated. So every day for the next few weeks, my mother endured the long trip from home to the hospital on public transport to express milk so that I was fed and nourished. Because I was quarantined in my heated Perspex box, there was very little physical contact between us. This deficiency of connection in those critical first weeks would set the tone for our future relationship.

I was discharged from Somerset Hospital once I had gained sufficient weight and the jaundice had receded from my skin, and was taken to our family home in Ocean View. The house was my parents' first home. Established in 1968 by the apartheid government and to which the non-white residents of nearby suburbs were forcibly removed, under the regime's Group Areas Act, Ocean View was the farthest conceivable suburb in the South Peninsula, and – adding insult to the entire low-income community's throbbing injury – had absolutely no view of the ocean from anywhere in the neighbourhood.

Before gathering enough finances to set up their own house, my parents had lived with my paternal grandmother, Ma Gladys, in a cramped dwelling in Bridgetown in Athlone. My father's grandmother, Big Mommy – who was paradoxically a tiny, hunched-over, permanently scowling woman – did not approve of my mother for reasons known only to her. This discomfort ensured that it wasn't long before they hastily pooled their money and bought the house in Hercules Road, Ocean View.

My parents had met at the Eureka Hotel in Elsie's River in 1969. My mother's cousin had set them up on a blind date before the term 'blind date' even existed. My mother, already 34 years old and still living at home with her mother in Upper Queens Road, Walmer Estate, was a classic beauty. Fine featured, porcelain skin with a sleek curtain of long, straight hair and always fashionably dressed, she loved nothing more than to dance. Her chosen style was wild and dripping with sex appeal. She could also, because of her skin tone, "pass for white" especially in the darkened halls of local dances at the Civic Centre – a Whites-Only building that she made sure she left before the lights came on, an act that was both brazen and illegal. She often bragged about her father, grandfather and extended family being white ("We're related to the Malans, you know …" – a dubious badge of honour) but this did not allow her to change the racial classification indelibly printed in her Identity Book though she would most certainly have passed the notorious 'pencil test'. The all-knowing pencil would have slid smoothly through her silky hair which, when wrapped in brown paper, soaked in vinegar and ironed flat on the ironing board by one of her sisters, reached all the way down to her bum.

My father, who was 31 at the time, possessed masses of charm, was always immaculately dressed and was also a legitimate ladies' man. He was from mixed stock – as were most coloured people: St Helena Island and traces of Cape Malay – so his taut brown skin was in sharp contrast to my mother's light pallor.

Later my father was to say that he felt deceived by my mother and had thought that she was taller than she actually was as she had towered over his five-foot-two frame in her shiny new high heels. In stockinged feet she was actually slightly shorter than him.

When she met my father, my mother was on a harrowing, lengthy rebound. Her fiancé (not her first) had been killed in an accident while working on the ships shortly before their wedding. She mourned and cried for what seemed like an eternity; then one day her tears dried up, and she resolved to never let her emotions get the better of her again. She also began actively despising effusive emotional displays in others.

My mother and I would turn out to be a match made in feelings hell.

My parents' courtship spanned two and a half years, with my mother controlling the purse strings and dispensing a R10-a-week allowance to my father for expenses and travelling by public transport from work or Bridgetown, where he still lived with his mother, Ma Gladys. Ma Gladys had never married my father's biological father, Barnie de Vries; neither did she marry the father of his half-brother, and so she stoically raised the two boys alone, which was scandalous and unheard of during those times.

My parents got married, as was the custom in the early 1970s, because it was the "done thing". Although my mother was the middle child of seven children, she was the last to marry. They exchanged vows at the local courthouse on a blistering day in February 1972 as is attested by the dark sweat stains under the armpits of all those present in the official black-and-white wedding photographs. Both of them are smiling broadly with their respective sets of perfect dentures, but there is a distinct and noticeable absence of chemistry or loving exchanges.

Two years to the date, my brother entered the world; and not long after, I, the unplanned mistake, was born. I do not, of course, remember my own birth. The world itself only really came into clear Technicolour focus around my fourth birthday. Before that day, life was a mono-tonal blur of the unknown, glimpses of uncertain reality and deeply suppressed memories.

Ocean View remains shrouded in mystery to me. I have pieced together memories from old photographs and other people's anecdotes and have stitched my recollections onto others', as one does squares on a patchwork quilt. I remember running my fingers through the prickly fur of a dog, an Alsatian. I remember the back of my thighs rubbing against a scratchy brown-and-yellow couch. I remember hugging my brother and the feel of the soft blue woollen cardigan he wore. I remember lying on my mother's chest, pretending to be asleep, in the passenger seat on a drive home, before it was mandatory to wear seatbelts. And I remember a hand, large and strong, holding mine firmly and leading me into a small room.

Then nothing.

CHAPTER 2

Dirty Little Secret

It would be many years later that the secrets, hidden so deeply, would erupt so violently and flood my frontal lobe. I would remember the hand and to whom it belonged: a trusted male family member. I would remember what came after. But long before that, at the age of four, I did not consciously know that I was the chosen keeper of such unspeakable secrets.

Where do secrets live? Do they reside in the sacred heart, encased in the living tissue awash with precious lifeblood? Do they find a resting place on the soft pillows of the lips, waiting to be whispered to the ears of expectant lovers or trusted confidantes? Or do they find shelter in the darkest depths of the mind, closeted away even from ourselves for fear of ever alluding to the terrifying truth? Or do secrets insinuate their way into the flesh, as they did with me at the age of four, commandeering every cell of my tiny body and betraying an awful certainty, of which I had no cerebral memory and that my tongue could not yet articulate.

The insistent memory of my sexual abuse found its way to my chubby fingertips in the middle of the night, as I lay alone under the itchy eiderdown in my single wooden bed across the room from my brother's. My probing digits slid into my floral cotton pyjama pants and located my unusually over-stimulated clitoris. I marvelled at the deep pleasure-pain sensation that touching myself elicited. The feeling was not entirely unfamiliar. I rubbed myself roughly and groaned quietly, as the bed creaked noisily beneath my shifting weight, then gasped as I climaxed – although I was only to learn that this is what had physiologically occurred much later on – and then I was immediately filled with immense shame, confusion and overwhelming guilt. I withdrew my hands quickly from my pyjamas and rolled over in my bed and faced the bumpy, cold concrete wall and sobbed heavily and quietly. This would be my compulsive routine for many years to follow.

Some nights I would intermingle and fuel the furtive masturbation with rich, detailed fantasies: some snatched from television scenes not intended for children's eyes, some from my own vivid imaginings, all with the same themes of submission and secrecy. Sometimes my mother, who had never acknowledged something as indulgent as the rights of children to their privacy, would catch me in the act. These intrusions would be utterly mortifying, made worse still by the dire warning she always issued that "it was dirty" and my "hands would fall off" if I carried on "doing *that*". I felt brutally shamed and burned with humiliation; I also began regularly checking that my hands were still attached to my arms by shaking them almost violently at my sides until the pain in my wrists was almost too much to bear.

By now I was four years old and we had just moved from Ocean View to Fairways, a small suburb on the fringes of the Cape Flats right at the very end of the M5 highway; the last bastion of the coloured middle class in Cape Town. A single road separated Fairways from the abject poverty and council-erected flats of the suburb of Parkwood, but that road was an invisible boundary that represented measurable class, wealth and culture. My father had obtained a job as a sales representative at a liquor company. Almost every second household's father in that neighbourhood worked as a rep, either for a liquor or tobacco company. Fairways' swimming pools, manicured gardens, shiny cars and private-school fees were funded almost entirely on the back of booze and nicotine. My father's position in the company would later give rise to his infamous justification that it was "his job to drink". He always drove around with at least six cases of Red Heart Rum in the boot of his car, either to give away to others or for personal consumption. The pungent aroma of that dark, sticky spirit, either on someone's breath or in half-filled glasses, filled the cracks of my childhood.

My father had many close, personal friends. He was so well connected that he was able to procure just about anything: alcohol, crayfish, perlemoen, good deals on cars, building materials, anything. Everyone knew him, everyone liked him. He was charismatic, affable and exceedingly generous – especially when he had been drinking. For years I would be known not by my first name but as "Alfie Martin's daughter".

I remember the first morning, a Saturday, after moving into our three-bedroomed house, complete with lurid orange fitted kitchen, L-shaped lounge, dining room with fireplace, front and back garden and garage. The air was crisp and clean and smelled of freshly mowed grass. My brother and I peered out from around the front gate of the walled garden into the wide street that was devoid of hurtling cars and meandering foot traffic, so commonplace in our previous neighbourhood. We edged our way to the threshold of the driveway and sat on the curb, hugging our knees, and just waited. For what, we were unsure.

An eternity passed.

We dug up the sand in the gutter.

We interfered with a line of marching ants on the pavement. I tore up some leaves.

My brother untied, then retied his shoelace, then tied the two separate laces to each other, then untied them again.

And then, sweet salvation. From the house diagonally opposite, a lanky, dark-skinned boy appeared from atop a yellow-white mound of sand that seemed to have been dumped hastily on the front lawn. He waved. I looked at my brother, who returned the look and nodded. Yes, he was waving at us. We raised our arms and signalled a greeting, slowly, in response. The boy scrambled nimbly down the small dune and raced across the street towards us without checking for cars. I was awe-struck at his brazen fearlessness. He skidded to a halt just in front of us.

"I'm Robin," he offered the introduction to my brother. He appeared younger, but was slightly taller, with dark shiny skin, curly brown hair and soft brown eyes.

"I'm Alcid-John," my brother AJ volunteered. As always, this introduction was met with a mixture of semi-confusion and resignation. Robin crinkled his nose, then shrugged his shoulders and decided to move on. He looked down at me.

"Oh," added my brother, almost apologetically, "this is my sister." Robin nodded. I nodded, accepting that "my sister" was all the introduction I was going to be afforded for now.

"Let's go play."

And with those words, we knew instantly we belonged.

That day we made metaphorical mountains out of the molehill of construction sand on Robin's parents' front lawn, digging and sliding and burying and balling up fistfuls of the gritty granules and showering each other with it until we were crunching it between our teeth and shaking it out of our socks and shoes. We spent hours playing with just the sand and each other and it was exhilarating and exhausting. When I took a bath that night, I dug the coarse silt from out of my ears, my belly button and other crevices until the bottom of the bathtub resembled a shallow seabed. I was ecstatic to have had a normal day of wild, happy play. For once.

Because while the other neighbourhood children would play games such as Cops and Robbers, emulating their favourite television programme in imaginary role-plays in the warm, tarred streets, I was to be found coercing my young playmates into subversive, elaborate setups of Doctor-Doctor and Housey-Housey in our converted garage, which invariably involved an element of sexual experimentation and semi-nudity.

"Don't tell your mommy and daddy!" I made them promise, pressing my index finger firmly to their lips while always keeping a watchful eye on the door. Urgently whispered words I had heard before, that I repeated so effortlessly, yet so robotically, though I didn't know where I had learned them.

When my parents went to work and my brother to school

during the week, I was left in the care of our neighbour, Auntie Edna. She was not my real aunt. I grew up in a time where all older females were Auntie and all older males were addressed as Uncle, as a sign of respect. So I had many, many uncles and a glut of aunties, whether I liked it or not. Some were actual blood relatives, some were neighbours, and some just delivered the black bags full of illegally caught perlemoen or came to install the burglar bars.

During naptime at Auntie Edna's, I would be laid down to sleep with great difficulty in her teenage daughter's garishly decorated bedroom. I fought sleep during the day as much as I did at night; I was terrified and anxious being alone in that pink, purple and red room that threatened to swallow me whole. I hated that the bedroom door, plastered with posters of pop idols and a Japanese cartoon character with too-big eyes that stated, "Love is ... never having to say you're sorry", was closed. When I shut my eyelids, I felt a surge of electricity course through and jolt my little body. I clenched my tiny teeth so hard I thought I might crack them. The only thing that ever helped was when I stuffed a small beanbag doll belonging to the teenage daughter down into my cotton panties and nestled it close to my *cookie*. It felt so comforting. I felt so safe. I eventually fell asleep. When I awoke from my nap, the doll would always be lying next to me on the pillow and, curious and slightly ashamed, I would wonder who had found it and removed it from its hiding place.

I had discovered the videotape while playing hide-and-seek with my brother one morning during his school holidays. It had been stashed away in the back of my father's clothes cupboard, which smelled of rubber soles, polyester and stale Old Spice. The writing scrawled horizontally across the label of the Betamax video cassette read *Little Girl Blue* so my expectation as I stuffed it into the video machine and waited ages for it to rewind was that tinny voiced, animated figures would spring to life on the large-tube television screen and start singing nursery rhymes. So I was more than a little surprised when a large Technicolour vagina filled the screen instead. The picture was fuzzy and jumpy but unmistakable. It was definitely a vagina. And there was definitely a man's tongue licking it.

I was no stranger to the idea of 'blue movies'. My father and his friends watched them at our house on Saturday afternoons from time to time. I would sneak glimpses through the vinyl concertina door that separated our tiled entrance hall from the lounge where they screened the movies. My mother would shoo me away from my Peeping Tom position and then go back to kitchen where she would continue making snacks for our visitors. But I had never really seen anything like this.

The images of what I would later understand to be graphic, lurid oral sex scenes were seared instantaneously into my brain and were to remain there for perpetuity. They would colour my fantasy life as a child and fuel my real sex-life later on.

I watched five minutes of the movie, transfixed, before my brother walked in on me. I hurriedly ejected the tape and ran down the passage and returned it to the cupboard, behind the piles of worn shoes. I waited every day for a few stolen minutes to remove the cassette from its hiding place and watch those few scenes; sometimes I would sit cross-legged on the scratchy carpet, my nose mere centimetres from the screen; other times I would kick up the footrest of my father's Lay-Z-Boy and sink into its folds while touching myself, coming all too soon from being exceedingly over-stimulated.

Then one day, when I went to retrieve the video cassette, it was gone. I tossed all the shoes out and searched every inch of the cupboard but couldn't find it. At first, I felt huge disappointment. but then came the fear and deep humiliation.

Someone – who, my parents – knew my secret. I wondered whether they were going to say anything. Was I in trouble? Were they going to explain what it was that I had seen? Were they going to finally make sense of everything that had been happening to me?

But no one said a word. I soon learned that this was how it worked in my family.

We Never Talked About Things. Ever.

We Always Pretended Everything Was Okay.

CHAPTER 3

The Age of Consent

Sexual abuse doesn't necessarily mean penetrative sex. I only read that when I was in my thirties in an alarming but revelatory book given to me by my therapist. But up until then, the myriad experiences I had that did actually fall under the banner of abuse were pushed aside, swept away into a dark corner of denial and excuses. That's to say, I made excuses for *them*. I felt like I'd been the one doing something wrong; that I had provoked it or brought it on myself.

"Don't be so silly," the adults would chorus. "He's only joking!"

I was six years old when it began. He was my Uncle Edward – the husband of my mother's sister – and every time we visited their childless home, I made sure I wore trousers. On the rare occasion that I absent-mindedly forgot or when my mother forced me to wear a dress for a special event such as a birthday or Christmas or just because she could tell me what to wear, I would arrive at their house anxious and apprehensive. I hated frilly, flouncy, itchy dresses anyway. I did gymnastics and athletics. I wanted to swing on the rusty washing line poles in their back yard and do cartwheels and handstands – which I could do for almost three minutes and for which I won an award at gymnastics for beating the entire squad. As I greeted my uncle with a compliant, obligatory kiss, he would grab a corner of the skirt of my dress and lift it up a few centimetres or more.

"Are you wearing panties today?" he would ask, his eyes twinkling with mirth, his eyebrows arched with malignancy.

I would tug my skirt back down violently and shy away from his crooked index finger.

He would follow me.

"I'm just checking … Beryl, is she wearing panties?" he would ask my mother or no one in particular and he would raise the skirt of my dress even higher, revealing my cotton underwear. I would cry then, ashamed and embarrassed. He, they, would laugh.

"Don't be so silly," they'd chorus. "He's only joking!"

My cousins taunted me, calling me a "cry baby". My mother gave me 'The Look', a non-verbal directive to behave myself, and stop embarrassing her. She and her sisters had inherited that unspoken eyeballing from my Ma Eileen. 'The Look' could stop any wayward child from moving or breathing – or, in my case, crying – from 20 paces. So I ran to the spare bedroom while the merriment continued in other parts of the house.

I must remember to not wear dresses. I must remember to not wear dresses. It's my fault for wearing a dress. He's only joking. He's only joking. I'm taking it all too seriously. I'm being silly. It's my fault. It's my stupid fault.

In that same year the inappropriate skirt-lifting started, my older cousin entered my room one Sunday afternoon, a towel wrapped around the waist of his lanky body. The fine baby hairs on my arms rose up and I just knew.

I don't know what or how, but I just knew.

He was probably 14, pushing through into semi-manhood, a faint moustache already sprouting on his upper lip and his voice cracking on occasion when he spoke too fast. I had just taken a shower and was sitting on my bed, also wrapped in a towel, still smelling of chlorine and ineffectual sunblock. My mother made me lather myself with thick, white sunscreen because she hated it when I "burned black" in summer. She was vocal in her disapproval of my skin tone darkening. It made me, she said, "look like a *kaffir* child".

As my cousin drew closer to my bed, I pushed myself up against the wall, cold where my shoulders were exposed.

"Show me," he said. It wasn't a question.

I pulled my towel tighter around my shivering body.

"You show me yours and I'll show you mine," he said matter-of-factly.

"No," I managed through chattering teeth, " I don't want to."

He dropped his towel to the floor, revealing a flaccid adolescent penis, balls shrivelled up from either the cold or the fear.

"Now it's your turn."

I knew this wasn't childish experimentation. He was old enough to have sex, to have seen vaginas his own age, to do what I had seen on the video.

I shut my eyes tightly. "No, I don't want to."

Closing my eyes might have been my undoing because I felt my towel being pulled roughly open at the bottom where it had rested on my thighs. I pushed my knees together but felt his hands prying them apart.

Hours passed. Or perhaps just minutes.

When I opened my eyes again, he had donned his own beach towel and was leaving the room.

"Thanks," he said.

"Thank you," I found myself muttering, wincing as I spoke the words.

It would be decades before I realised or even partially remembered that these were blatant acts of abuse. These situations, as well as the time that older man slid his hands under my school skirt and in between my thighs after paying for my banana split at Milky Lane where I went at the end of every term, to celebrate, by myself; or when that man in the row in front of me turned and stared at me while vigorously masturbating when I went to see *Dirty Dancing* at The Luxurama; or when my GP moaned quietly while performing an internal exam to see if I had miscarried; or when the energy healer unbuttoned my jeans without my permission or when the hungover local at the campsite in Istanbul pulled my towel from my naked body and felt up my breasts because he had shared his raki with us the night before; or the times when I was actually raped but couldn't even put that word to it because I was too emotionally numb to defend or take care of myself.

Hashtag. Me too.

CHAPTER 4

Don't Swim After Eating

The year I decided to grow up and assume control over my life, I received 15 surgical stitches in my right foot and second-degree burns across my chest. I was six and three quarter years old.

I had scrutinised the primary caretakers in my life with an eagle eye; I had assumed the role of a lesser-bumbling Inspector Clouseau, that detective in *The Pink Panther*, just not quite so incompetent. We were clothed, we were fed, we wanted for nothing materially – in fact, people called us "spoilt". They called us "Super Coloureds". We had a nice house, a new car every second year; we went on luxurious holidays to the casinos in the independent homelands. My childhood was littered with trips to Sun City and the Wild Coast Sun. We hardly ever saw our parents as they were gambling from after the continental buffet breakfast until midnight when they could gain access to the money in their accounts again via the ATMs. Resort Kids' Clubs were made for children like us. Casino orphans. With signing power.

Early on, I knew something, many things, were sinisterly amiss in the perfect paint-by-numbers façade of our home.

It was a hot, sweaty, bloody day. That broken glass should never have been there.

The shattered glass was like the battered-in bit of the bedroom door, the droplets of dried blood on the headboard, the cracked kitchen window, the haunting coffee stain on the dining-room wall and the other assorted battlefield debris that could be found scattered around my parents' house, displayed like pyrrhic trophies.

These wartime fragments were unspoken reminders to others of my parents' mutual unhappiness in their marriage, just in case it wasn't already blatantly obvious. These broken bits and pieces remained unfixed for as long as was tolerable or depended on whether we would have visitors coming that following weekend. Sometimes it took days to dispose of or repair; sometimes years, as was the fate of the bedroom door.

The visible wreckage of their passive-aggressive violence pierced through the otherwise perfect pretence of our suburban lives. Their reciprocal message was unmistakable:

This wasn't over.

And it wasn't. It seemed eternal, trapped in that wrecked perfection.

Like secretly touching myself, I felt enormous guilt about that yellow-brown coffee stain.

On a Saturday morning, a month before the broken glass, I had been very whiney and vocal about the hardened state of the yolk of my fried egg. I could not stand the rubbery texture of hard egg yolks. They made me gag. To be fair, I had a problem with most food textures and was always a very picky eater. I was often the last at the dining table, forced to clear the contents of my plate despite continued protestations about the sliminess of mushrooms, the bittiness of desiccated coconut and, of course, rubbery eggs.

My mother unceremoniously advised me to, "Eat my fucking egg."

My father had then adroitly picked up his amber coffee cup by its ear and thrown the steaming contents into my mother's face.

"I hate the way you talk to the children!" he had yelled, then sat down to resume eating.

The sticky droplets of the too-sweet coffee had clung to my

mother's fine light-brown hair then ran slowly down her creaseless forehead and into her eyes, which shone with a mixture of rage and shock. She did not move to wipe it from her face.

She pursed her lips tightly, shot a venomous look in my direction, then turned silently away, pushing through the wooden saloon-style swing doors to the kitchen. My brother started moving a suddenly fascinating piece of toast around his plate with his fork, mopping it up with some luridly red tomato sauce, which he then put in his mouth and chewed soundlessly.

What remained was a dripping splatter on the wall where my humiliated mother had been standing. While my stomach churned with distress and shame, I remembered wondering how long the stain would remain there.

Two weeks.

That coffee splatter watched me accusingly every morning as I ate my watery ProNutro for two long weeks before I finally cleaned it off ruefully with my own spit and a snotty tissue I kept balled up in my gown pocket.

But a month later, on that blistering day, the glass was there, where it shouldn't have been. That semi-smashed drinking tumbler, still stained with the last party's rum and Coke, minding its own business in the blazing December sun.

My brother chased me around the paved yard with the looping green hosepipe, letting out whoop-whoops along the way. He pushed his thumb over the nozzle and a stream of water shot out, forming a hard arcing spray in my direction.

We had all been swimming after lunch, which was already quite a precarious move considering the well-known rule that you should not swim after you eat. All the adults said so. I had just carefully towelled off and was sunning myself on the toasty red bricks and was in no mood to get wet again. Seeing the imminent danger, I rose quickly from my sun-tanning position and bolted. AJ raced across the back garden in hot pursuit, dodging sunburned cousins and shrivelled pool noodles. We ran around the swimming pool, him brandishing the treacherous rubber hose. I screamed a few choice profanities as I sprinted away, words I had picked up from the drunken dialogue of reckless adults and of which I didn't actually know the precise meaning. Except 'fuck'. Leigh-Ann Klein had told me what *that* meant during second break.

I grabbed the rusty washing line pole and swung around it to escape the threatening jet stream. He saw it first. He dropped the rubber hose; it snaked around the yard demonically. Like a slow-motion Saturday-morning cartoon character, my brother's mouth opened and closed mechanically but no sound came out.

I looked down to see that a massive shard of glass had slashed through the sole of my right foot and the sharpened sliver now protruded out through the top, exposing white bone. A tide of my own thick crimson blood spread rapidly out across the cement courtyard and flowed towards my father's prize dahlias and roses.

It was only then that I let out a piercing scream that reverberated through my tiny skull and was, I was later told, heard by the entire neighbourhood.

A few months later, I obtained second-degree burns across the left side of my chest. I had been lying on the black vinyl bench that formed part of a lurid orange U-shaped breakfast nook in the kitchen. The bench rose up to form a counter on which stood the toaster and the kettle. I reached out – one hand on the table, one on the counter – to hoist myself up. My right hand connected with a freshly boiled kettle and I pulled it and its scalding contents down onto my chest.

I don't remember much else except being in the lounge, sitting incongruously calmly on Auntie Edna's lap while a paramedic carefully placed orange gunk and gauze on the burn. I looked past what seemed like a curious, anxious crowd and saw my brother in the arms of our neighbour's daughter. He was bawling and spluttering.

"Don't let my sister die! Don't let my sister die!"

Blood. Tears. Chaos. Trauma.

I decided then that it was time to look after myself.

As hard as they may have been trying, the adults in my life were doing a fucking shit job.

CHAPTER 5

Black and White

I stopped. I jammed my index finger into the back of my mouth and tried to pry the globby sweet out of my back teeth. It was definitely stuck. The midday commuters rushed past me, unaware of my battle with the Wilson's toffee. I sucked down hard against my palate then probed the sticky mass with the tip of my tongue.

Damn, this sweet was going to last forever.

"Desiree-Anne!" My mother had noticed my absence at her side. "Hurry up! We're going to miss the train."

I quickened my pace and hurried to meet her. Even in her six-inch stilettos, my mother's stride was quick and purposeful. She always wore high heels. In fact, the higher the better. She had a corner cupboard in the bedroom devoted exclusively to her shoes, boxes stacked from floor to ceiling of the most glamorous footwear I had ever seen.

Every third Saturday, a man came around to the house with blue-and-white boxes with black lids bearing the name 'Indigo'. Inside were yellow, sequinned, leather, feathered shoes, any kind you could conjure. Their commonality lay in their daring spiked heels. My mother would slip her calloused feet with their polished toenails into those shoes and ask, "What do you think, baby?" and I, seated cross-legged on the lounge carpet, would always clap my hands with delight as she sashayed across the room. "Yes, those,

those!" I'd cheer, even if I didn't really like them because I was so taken aback at the very idea of being asked for my opinion.

And then, when my mother was outside waving goodbye to the shoe man, I would secretively slip my little feet into the new towering heels and shuffle unsteadily around the lounge, making the dog nervous. I loved these stolen, shaky moments in my mother's shoes. The uneasy feeling in my stomach, the ache in my calves. And then I would tumble from that dizzying height as I heard the front gate click shut to the return of my mother from seeing off Mr Goliath. I would place the shoes exactly as I had found them, refolding the tissue paper carefully and smoothing out the creases, then patting each shoe gently before replacing the lid.

It was black suede heels with a red trim that I hurried to keep up with that Wednesday lunchtime. They perfectly complemented the rest of my mother's outfit. They always did. A black woollen knitted twinset with a deep cherry-red three-quarter-length overcoat. Despite my mother's efforts, I always managed to look as though I had just rolled out of a charity donation bin. I plucked at my chunky knitted tights, gathering around my knees in folds. The strap of my checked pinafore slipped off my shoulder again as I hiked it up with my thumb.

I caught up with my mother and took her hand. It was soft and dry, the nails dark red and sharply manicured, contrasting against her fair skin. We walked down the sloping concourse towards Cape Town Station. The pavement was slippery from the recent downpour and steam rose up from the ground. I pushed my soles down and tried to make myself slide a little as I walked. My mother deftly jerked her arm to make me stop. I reluctantly obeyed.

I loved coming into the city. I loved not being at school. It was a good day.

The visit to the ear, nose and throat specialist had revealed that all were "working fine". It was a Big Deal because my mother had had to take off from work and we had to take the train because my father had Meetings.

When I was nearly two years old, my mother had thought me belligerent and naughty. My Ma Eileen had suspected I was a little deaf. A quick thwack of two hardcover copies of the *Reader's Digest* a little distance behind my head – and no noticeable reaction – had proven my Ma's diagnosis to be more accurate. Multiple surgeries followed to remove my tonsils and adenoids and have grommets inserted into my ears. But my hearing, especially in my left ear, would never be one hundred per cent. Especially when I didn't like what was being said.

The sounds of the city made my bones vibrate. The deep honks and shrill hoots of the urgent traffic. The melodic sales pitch of persuasive street vendors. The steady, buzzing drone of electricity coursing under my feet, above my head. The insistent footsteps of people going … where exactly? I wanted to know where they were going, with their rectangular faux-leather briefcases and damp, heavy coats. But we had a train to catch.

My mother showed our tickets to the man seated at the gate. He clipped them without looking and we passed through the turnstile into the large terminal. My mother located a schedule, affixed to a nearby face-brick pillar. She scanned it with her index finger, her finger hovering millimetres away from the grimy Perspex cover, then pronounced, "Two", and ushered me towards the platform. As we passed the train's engine, a man in a dark blue uniform stepped out of the door onto the platform and blew a whistle.

"Hurry up!" urged my mother. I broke into a half-run. We passed the open door of a carriage.

"Can't we get in this one?" I asked.

"No, no. Further down."

We jogged alongside the length of the maroon-and-silver train. The whistle blew piercingly again from behind us and the train let out a loud hiss from somewhere in its serpentine belly. Other people were now running down the platform too.

"This one!" yelled my mother and skilfully climbed up onto the step of a carriage. I followed, clambering up, grabbing her hand to do so. The carriage was half full and we shuffled down the aisle to find empty seats. My mother sank into a window seat. I took the seat opposite her.

"I'm hot. Can we open the window please, Mommy?" I asked.

"Sit down."

I sat down. I stood up.

"Can we open the window please?"

My mother looked in her handbag and withdrew her cigarettes and lighter. She lit a long, thin, white cigarette and, as she did, the shrill whistle blew again and the train lurched forward as though my mother had engineered its departure herself. My mother stood up and unlocked the window latch. The window dropped down suddenly. I jumped back and laughed. My mother sat back and sighed. I kneeled on the seat and craned my neck out the window. The train was starting to move. Another ear-splitting whistle.

"Look's like we just made it, Mommy."

The train begun picking up speed. We passed an industrial area, dirty and blackened with grime. I dropped back into my seat.

"I don't understand why we had to run all the way down to this carriage," I said.

My mother regarded me for a few seconds then replied, "Different people have to sit in different carriages." She looked out the window but seemed as though she was looking even farther away.

"What do you mean?" I asked, leaning forward, "Different how?"

She took another deep drag on her cigarette, then exhaled. She leaned forward and whispered conspiratorially, "There are different carriages. First class in the front of the train, third-class carriages at the end."

I blinked, knitted my brow and waited for a further explanation. It came. But this time my mother's tone was more reproachful.

"Well, if you weren't so dark," she said, "we'd be able to sit up front in the Whites-Only carriages."

I flinched and shut my eyes tightly as though I had been struck across the face. When I opened them again, my entire Technicolour world had changed to black and white.

CHAPTER 6

Playing with Dolls

I hated that doll. That much was clear in my radically abusive treatment of it. I often yanked the head right off the body and subjected it to a myriad of homespun experiments to test its hardiness. I cut half of its hair off and left the other half matted against the side of its plastic skull, after administering a vigorous scrubbing with a bar of Sunlight soap and a Dettol concoction I had brewed up in a old ice-cream *bakkie* in the bathroom.

I had wanted a Baby Angel First Love doll for as long as I could remember. I had seen a friend's prized doll at ballet class and felt overwhelming jealousy and utter adoration for its blue eyes and lashed lids that opened and closed when you put her to sleep. I loved that you could feed her a bottle – even though it was obviously fake – and that she peed just like a real baby. I also loved the squeezable soft plastic, silky smooth to the touch. I wanted to have it and own it and worship it forever.

As the sun rose on my eighth Christmas morning, I manically clawed at the gaudy wrapping paper, nearly hyperventilating from excitement. I gasped and spluttered when I saw the contents of the box. I dropped it to the carpeted floor as though it had scalded my little fingers.

What the ...?

The doll was all *wrong*! The doll had *black* skin!

This was not what I had wanted at all. Its skin was black! As black as the frightful night. As black as the mole on Ma Eileen's neck. As black as the ace of spades. It's hair was also black and curled up into a deplorable Afro of sorts. This was just *all* wrong!

I had huge trouble reconciling this silicone tar baby with the idea I had of myself in my head. When I scrunched my eyes closed, I imagined myself a pretty princess with clear, white porcelain skin, dimpled cheeks and flowing blonde hair. Like Barbie. And the girls on TV. There were no girls like me on the censored, embargoed televisions unless you counted Rudy Huxtable from *The Cosby Show* and she was just so sweet and perfect and as cute as a button you could choke on. In fact, the Huxtables were the only people of colour on TV: upper class, one parent a doctor and the other a lawyer, well-behaved kids and moralistic half-hours to which we stayed glued weekly. The only thing Rudy's parents, Bill and Claire, ever did when she made a dent in their highly principled lives was say – in unison –"Oh, Rudy!" and roll their eyes and everyone would fall about in fits of canned laughter. Rudy was not like me. Though her hair resembled mine, her life was not like mine at all.

I was confused; my image in the mirror in the inside of my mother's cupboard contradicted my imaginings. I was short and squat, even for my age, with chubby thighs and a round, ample butt, which my mother referred to as "Bushman bums". My hair was coarse and mad, and defied hair bands and pretty clips. That morning – because it was Christmas – my mother recklessly and painfully combed out my thick, candyfloss hair and tugged it into tight, perfectly symmetrical plaits that started above my ear. She secured them with red bobbles, round elastics with plastic orbs on the ends that I occasionally whipped around over my shoulders and sucked on when I was bored. My hair was always a contentious issue with my mother. She had fair, fine, straight hair. My hair was unruly and rebellious, and on special occasions had to be plastered down with Brylcreem. Throughout the years to come, my hair would undergo a variety of attempts to achieve sleek, straight perfection. The tugging and painful pulling of round brushes as the heat of scorching hairdryers singed my ears and my scalp. The chemical straighteners that, at one stage, made all the hair on the front of my head fall out. Colourful, round plastic curlers secured with lethal white plastic pins that dug into my skull and had to be worn for almost an entire day to achieve any resemblance to straight hair. Curl your hair to straighten it: a counter-intuitive process if ever there was one.

"You have to suffer to be beautiful, Desiree-Anne," my mother constantly reminded me. And, of course, I wanted to be beautiful so I endured the painful journey to acceptable prettiness.

At one stage, because I loved swimming and my mother hated constantly having to wash and dry my long, unmanageable hair, she took me to the hairdresser and instructed her to "cut it all off". I hadn't been consulted and watched tearfully as all my bushy locks collected in piles on the hairdresser's floor. I emerged looking like a little boy, resembling my brother somewhat, a curly-haired version of him, he who had inherited my mother's fair locks.

"It'll grow back," my mother promised ruefully – which it did, like wild *dagga*. So I was dragged off to the hairdresser again. Hack, hack. Snip, snip.

My grandmother called the wayward fluff that often escaped from their ponytail prisons *anoster bossies*: wild bushes, not a cultural term of endearment evidently. She frequently and habitually tried to flatten my flyaway hair with the palm of her hand. My hair could not deny my heritage.

The reality was that this doll was a scaled-down version of me, but it was not a version of who I wanted to be, who I had been led to believe it was better to be. White was better than Black. That's what I had learned. That's what I had overheard in adult conversations. That's what I saw on the grainy images on television. White people got more, had much more money, lived in special neighbourhoods just for them, got to go to places designated specifically for them, such as parks and beaches and ice-cream shops.

And so I proceeded to mercilessly torture the doll, just for having the wrong skin colour and the wrong hair. Just for being completely *wrong*. For being like me.

CHAPTER 7

The Prodigal Son Leaves

Events often happened in the wrong order in my childhood. For instance, I didn't get an additional brother in the normal way. He just arrived one day with an overstuffed faux-embroidered suitcase and a plastic carrier bag tied closed with a knot. And he was older than both AJ and I, a gangly, unformed version of my father. He had my dad's short, curly hair and brown skin and broad smile. We were told he was our brother; that his name was Brendon. We were told that my father had been married to another woman before my mother. We were told she was Muslim. I eyed this new sibling with suspicion, acutely aware of my parents' prejudice against the *"Slamse"*. Them and *"Kaffirs"*. They only talked about them derogatorily, though, when their actual Muslim friends weren't around, friends like Uncle Himma who often came over to play cards until the early hours of the morning. My parents didn't have any black friends.

One day my mother, embarrassed to her core, shouted at me when I walked out into the lounge where a smoky card game was taking place and offered everyone present microwaved bacon sandwiches. She shot up from her seat and ushered me back into the kitchen.

"We don't do that!" she shouted and whispered simultaneously. It was an amazing talent she possessed; to berate us without appearing to.

"Do what?" I asked.

"Talk about bacon in front of Uncle Himma."

"I'm sure he's heard the word before, Ma."

"That's not the point," she shifted to her aggravated whisper voice. "Just don't."

She pivoted and exited the kitchen and I proceeded to make a microwaved bacon sandwich for myself. I ate it in the kitchen lest the presence of bacon in the same room as Uncle Himma should cause an allergic, religious reaction of untold proportions.

My bother Brendon ate bacon. And pork, and most other pig products. He also quietly bullied my other brother, who wasn't one to complain about being pinched or shoved or verbally abused. And so the victimisation began. It would have been appropriate for him to tease and torment me, the youngest, but my brother was considerably weaker. He had suffered seizures almost his entire life and his disposition was gentle and non-confrontational. We walked on eggshells with AJ for fear of him collapsing in an epileptic fit. When he did seize, my dad or mom would then grab him by one leg and hang him upside down and smack his behind until he "came right". It was wholly traumatic for everyone, especially AJ, I imagine. And not something I think modern physicians would recommend in the treatment of epilepsy.

Brendon would be sweet as honey in the company of the adults, a proficient teenage sycophant. He particularly tried to ingratiate himself with my father – his father – but my mother would block every attempt. I think my mother suspected that Brendon was not behaving in the manner required of someone who was graciously taken into another woman's house. Their relationship was icy, at best. And their best was positively glacial.

Brendon slept in the spare room, which I thought was appropriate as he always had an air of spare-ness about him; like he didn't quite fit in, like there were no relationships in the entire family that anchored him to our world. The room was aptly named as it held a single bed and an assortment of miscellaneous clutter, cardboard boxes and unopened suitcases. It was here that Brendon would unleash his subtle terror on my brother. He would be merciless. He'd pinch, shove and hit AJ; grasp his medically fragile body in a headlock and rub his head vigorously with his knuckles.

Although a girl and two years younger than him, I was the one blessed with the high pain threshold. AJ yelped from pain. He tried to wriggle free but Brendon was older and stronger than him and wrestled him onto the bed. Hot tears ran down his cheeks. That was my signal: I leapt up off the blue padded vinyl chair and launched my entire self at Brendon, knocking AJ free whilst slamming Brendon into the bedroom wall. He screamed out in pain as his head connected with the wall. AJ fell to the floor, still crying. I landed on my side of the bed, breathless and more than a little victorious.

My mother burst in, beckoned by the battle cries of warfare.

"What's going on here?" she demanded.

My father was behind her in seconds. We all went dead quiet.

"What is going on here?"

AJ broke the silence. Principles and morals in abundance, he felt compelled to tell the truth. "B-b-rendon's been hurting me."

I was deeply disappointed that he did not mention my radical and heroic rescue.

My mother looked back over her shoulder at my father who was wearing the grimmest of expressions.

"He has to go," she said firmly.

My father did not disagree in any way. And just like that, within months of his arrival, I lost a brother.

CHAPTER 8

The Exits are Located to the Right

Losing a brother I barely knew hardly caused a dent in my heart. It was nothing like my grandmother, Ma Eileen's passing. I saw her die before she actually did. Not in the way that the rest of the family had seen her, at a huge farewell at the Departures Terminal at DF Malan Airport. She was jetting off on a round-the-world trip to visit all of the family living abroad. Her first stop was my Auntie Sandy in New York. The whole family had gathered to say goodbye at the airport. I was very excited because I got to leave school early.

If there was ever a consummate family matriarch, it was my grandmother, Eileen Solomon. Having raised seven children in a two-bedroomed house in Walmer Estate, rearing four girls and three boys through two world wars while her husband fought valiantly in both. She had inadvertently or directly passed on many superstitions and general codes of conduct. For example, one must always make one's bed in the morning. This particular rule derived from the time of rationings during the War. Ma Eileen had been queueing at the butchery to collect her paper parcels for the week when one of the butcher's assistants sawed his digits clean off with a meat saw. The sight of the dismembered metacarpal had led Eileen to pass out right on the tiled floor. Friends and neighbours had helped her up and accompanied her home and the entire time she had been thinking about how, in her haste to get to the rationing queue before sunrise, she had left her bed unmade. She was mortified that those who entered her house and urged her to lie down saw that the bed was a tangled mess of crumpled sheets and pillows. And so the rule was established and passed on from generation to generation: *Always make your bed just in case someone loses a finger.*

This wasn't the only habit or superstition she had passed on to her children, which my mother, in turn, with accompanying solemn warnings, foisted onto me.

If you drop a knife accidentally on the floor, a male visitor will arrive unannounced.

"Linker klinker regte slegter." If your left palm was itchy, you would receive money soon, but if your right palm itched, you would part with money.

As you enter a new year, make damn sure your laundry is done and your dishes are clean.

FHB or *Family Hold Back*. This instruction, issued at every social occasion, ensured that guests ate first and family members were to respectfully (and, in my case, hungrily) wait to eat – if there was any food left.

Step on a crack [in the pavement], *break your mother's back.*

If a light bulb flickers off then on again, someone is about to die.

Don't sleep with your shoes facing the bed, or spirits will stand in them and watch you sleep.

One I got from my father is that if you're having particularly bad dreams in which you feel like something is sitting on your chest and paralysing you, place a Bible next to your bed with an open scissors on top. I would later find out that I suffered from an actual condition (as did he) called 'sleep paralysis', but continued to whip the otherwise unused Bible out and lay the scissors on them for comfort and protection.

I was gravely afraid of the dark and found myself twisted up in excruciating torment as a result of night terrors and sleep paralysis on a regular basis. I would find solace in my parents' bed, creeping under the covers in between them like a mortified ninja. Until I was deemed to old, too big and unceremoniously evicted from their room. It was then that I started my bleary-eyed journey to chronic insomnia. The dark so scared the shit out of me that I chose to stay awake until the safety of the dawn or until I passed out, whichever came first.

I loved my Ma Eileen but she scared the shit out of me too. One of her more famous escapades saw her cracking a wooden breadboard in half on my mother's head for coming home past her curfew one night. But she was loving and had a dark sense of humour, yet she was stern and firm and didn't tolerate crap.

After school, AJ and I would walk the long trek from Zonnebloem Junior School up to her house in Upper Queens Road – carefully avoiding the corner café that swallowed our pocket money periodically – where she cared for us until our parents collected us after work. Her small semi-detached house was astounding. The main bedroom had a bed that folded up flush against the wall, a curtain hiding the springy bed.

We often played hide-and-seek behind those bobbled, woollen curtains though everyone knew that that was the most obvious hiding place. Or we hid under the sideboard where you'd have to squeeze in next to oversized seashells and ornate glass bowls. Her toilet had a string you had to pull to flush it, which I could reach standing on my tippy toes. Her kitchen table – where we were forced to do our homework – was pale blue-and-white laminate and had the most dizzying and distracting pattern on its surface.

The most frightening aspect of Ma Eileen's house was the steep slope of the road as you exited the front gate. We were often sent to the *babbie* shop next door and I always had to cling to the walls and slide my feet down the pavement to get to our destination where we could stock up on nigger balls and gobstoppers with the change we got from buying the milk and bread or bottles of Double "O" cool drink. I always feared that I would trip and fall and tumble all the way down Queens Road right into the harbour below.

The last photograph of me with my Ma sees her standing behind a baggage trolley at the airport, me at her side and my brother flanking her on the left. The very last thing I remember my Ma doing – our final exchange captured on celluloid for all eternity – is her trying to flatten my unmanageable bushy strands of hair that had escaped its plaits, as they always did.

But I saw her die; I knew she had died before everyone else did.

After we had seen her off, everyone gathered at our house for supper. Food is and will remain a central thread and staple of coloured culture. We eat. We make sure you eat. We make sure you have food to take home to eat.

I stood in the lounge and I saw her, my Ma, walk across the tiled entrance hall.

She wore a navy-blue-and-white dress and carried a navy blue handbag across her wrist. She stopped at the doorway, looked at me and smiled. Then she walked away. I told no one of my sighting. I had had several similar encounters throughout my childhood and the adults I told neither took me seriously nor nurtured my unusual gift. So I kept it to myself; malignant or horrifying, it was my mystical secret.

Half an hour after the sighting of my Ma, the phone rang. I raced to answer it because I loved answering the phone. The line was crackly and there was a delay. It was an overseas call.

"Can I speak to your father?"

It was my Auntie Sandy from New York.

"Hi, Auntie Sandy. How are you?" I asked enthusiastically. Overseas calls were rare and precious and exciting.

"Desiree-Anne, can I speak to your father?" And then I knew for sure Ma was dead.

I called my father to the phone and sat on the tiled floor, watching his face turn grim and his conversation become stilted, ending with, "I'll stay in touch. Thanks, Sandy."

I held my position on the cold tiles as my father made his way into the lounge to break the news that my grandmother had suffered a massive heart attack during the descent to New York. I heard the jovial sounds, the clinking of cutlery, the laughter of young cousins turn eerily silent as the tremor of the Most Terrible News carried through the house. And then there was crying. Not from everyone, of course. My mother did not cry as a rule, which is why she did not ever tolerate tears from her children. But other grown-ups wept openly, sobbed uncontrollably.

In that moment, the world felt entirely, unbearably empty and unsafe.

CHAPTER 9

State of Emergency

I felt perpetually unsafe, in my surroundings, within my own small, unstable realm.

There is another photograph of me, taken on the morning of my brother's first day of school. I'm standing in the garden, bare feet, in a blue-and-white sundress, wearing his school cap tilted at a jaunty angle and trying to hoist up his brown, boxy school bag in one hand. I am smiling, peering into the morning sun, but moments later I would be knee-deep in a uncontrollable paroxysm, wailing about the injustice of him being allowed to go to school and not me. That pervasive sense of injustice ran painfully deep and demonstratively in me. For years, I would throw vicious tantrums at the mere sniff of unfairness or become entirely histrionic at anything I perceived as discrimination.

It took two years before it was eventually my turn to attend Big School. I loved school and it loved me. My first day, I was called out for eating a cherry-red Zoo Animals lollipop during class and was utterly incensed because no one had explained the rules to me regarding eating times. Mrs Erentzen, my teacher, confiscated my half-sucked lollipop and dropped it ceremoniously in the metal bin, furthermore using me as an example of bad behaviour. I hated being in trouble. I felt physical pain whenever I was.

That day I also stole a book from the girl seated next to me. It was a learner's dictionary with colourful pages and big bold letters and I had to have it. So I slipped it out from her chair bag when no one was looking and deposited it into my school bag. When I got home that evening, I told my parents that the school had given a copy to every learner. They believed me. My career of crime shot straight out of the starting gates in Sub A.

I excelled at every subject and was constantly in competition with Yolanda Petersen who was a worthy opponent. She was smart, she was diligent; her hair, however, was even more *kroes* than mine. But I doubted that Yolanda had the ability to do what I did at the end of the academic year: I voluntarily agreed to perform a nursery rhyme in front of the entire school and teaching body at the end of year prize-giving. It never occurred to me not to.

On prize-giving day, I wore a red-and-white polka-dot dress that flared out at my knee, white lacy socks that came up to meet the edge of the dotty dress and my black 'tap shoes'. They were black patent-leather Mary-Janes that my mother had bought on account at Edgars but I wore them to dance furiously on the tiled entrance hall of our house, mimicking Mikhail Baryshnikov and Gregory Hines in *White Nights*.

Heel-toe. Heel-toe. Shuffle. Shuffle. Slide. Jazz hands.

Until my father yelled at me to stop, which was often. Because he had a crippling hangover. Which was more often.

I planted myself firmly on that rickety stage, in that vast crumbling hall, and delivered a show-stopping performance of 'Mary had a Little Lamb', with actions. I was brave, I was fearless; I did not care for the opinions of others. But I did love the subsequent rousing applause. My endearing passion for theatre was born.

Yolanda Petersen wasn't my only competition. At the end of every year, when the lime-green report cards were issued, my mother would withdraw my brother's report from a pink-and-white checked bag where she kept all the "important documents" and compare my grades to his from the same year to see who had done the best comparatively. Sibling rivalry simmered slowly in our family. Slowly, but potently and not very subtly. Perfectionism was prized. Excelling was extolled.

Except of course when I did well at something and my father would say, "I knew you would do well. We expected that." Defeated. Deflated. Ego wind right out of sails.

I loved my brother. What I despised was his flawless fragility. What I loathed was how everyone walked on eggshells around his supposed vulnerabilities while I was expected to be hardy and resilient. I resented that his life was devoid of applied pain while I got smacked sideways for being adventurous, for being unrelentingly curious. He was always a silent witness to my inflicted agony, a powerless protector. Like when my mother smacked my legs so hard for losing my school shoes. Her bare hands left white handprints inside the raised red-brown welting skin that I watched come up to meet me and recede again as we drove our bikes to the park in the spitting, drizzling summer rain. It had been his idea to take me there but I lead the way, crying, him pedalling quietly behind save for the squeaking of his unoiled bicycle chain. The park in Fairways was the most colourful and most treacherous landscape of my childhood; monstrously high fire-engine red slides and grass-green jungle gyms with the paint peeling off and unstable sunshine-yellow roundabouts and swings made from recycled tyres that hung from dizzyingly high poles. That park always presented a personal challenge and that day we slid down the impossibly long, searing hot dented metal sheeting of the slide, grazing our knees on the gravel landing strip and pulled ourselves up onto and swung from monkey bars, me fuelled by rage, him by pity. In later years, that park would be visited by myself and others for less innocent reasons. We could be found obliviously whiling away our misspent youths long after the sun had set and we would sit in those same swings, our knees now touching the ground, some smoking *majat* joints, others making out salaciously with their 'bad influences' under the slide, branding each other with 'love bites'. My brother would never go there. He was a good boy.

So I resented him. I wanted to hurt him because no one else dared to for fear he may die. So I did. I hurt him one evening. It was a silly game. I asked him to stretch out some tacky Prestik and told him I wanted to cut it with the bright orange Tallon kitchen scissors I'd procured from its holder on the kitchen wall. I had no intention of cutting the Prestik. Who does that? I aimed for and found the soft pad of the palm of his hand and sliced right through the flesh. At first there was no blood, then there was too much blood. He looked at me in horror, his eyes wide, but his pain was soundless. What happened next surprised me. He didn't run to my parents and rat me out. He ran, clutching his effusively bleeding hand, to the bathroom. I followed him and he pulled me inside, closing the door.

"I won't tell," he whispered. "It was an accident." He was protecting me.

We proceeded to wrap reams of toilet paper around the haemorrhaging hand. It looked like we were embalming a miniature mummy but the vivid red blood soaked right through our efforts. We unwrapped his hand and flushed the sticky toilet paper down the toilet. He held up his hand; a piece of flesh was dangling from his palm. We rewrapped the hand but it was useless: darkening blood and wrecked toilet paper everywhere.

There was a knock at the toilet door. We froze. Maybe they would go away? Another knock and the door flung open. My mother stood wide-eyed, surveying the sickening scene.

"What the fuck did you do?" She was directing the accusation at me as if only I could be capable of causing such violence.

I looked down at the floor. It was covered in blood splatters. I was going to be in a monumental pile of shit. It would hurt.

"It was an accident," said Alcid-John.

"Let's get you to the doctor," she ushered him out of the bloody crime scene.

I sat down on the toilet seat and started to cry. I had another reason to hate him.

I believed my internal nine-year-old chaos reflected my unbearable sensitivity to the mood of the time. It was 1985, and a State of Emergency had been declared by President PW Botha. He announced that violence in the country showed that "ordinary law and order was inadequate". By that time it was commonplace to see huge armoured vehicles – or Casspirs – patrolling the roads during the day, outside our school and in the streets.

It was a tense time made no less so by the detention of my 16-year-old cousin, Gareth, for public violence. This usually meant something as innocuous as throwing stones at those you shouldn't. The police came to fetch him and five other teenagers in the neighbourhood one night based on an anonymous tip-off. Gareth wasn't home so his parents, my aunt and uncle, had to fetch him from where he was and his dad then had to deliver him to Pollsmoor Prison. He was later transferred to Victor Verster Prison, near Paarl.

Two traumatic weeks followed. The adults spoke in hushed, anxious tones about care packages and incarceration and – as always – no one explained to the children what was actually happening. But I figured it out. A girl in my class's older brother had told me what detention was one day when I swore blind I had been hit on the hand by a rubber bullet on the walk to her house after school.

Detention – a fancy word for imprisonment without even the most basic human rights – was terrifying. People died without explanation. People just never came back.

When we visited my aunt and uncle, armed with prison-regulation food parcels and unspoken fear, my aunt had a huge bouquet of fresh flowers on the dining room table that had been brought to the mother of every detainee in the neighbourhood by the sister of two brothers who had been imprisoned. I felt guilt-ridden for thinking how beautiful they looked and smelled. A life for some cut flowers; it hardly seemed like a fair exchange.

Finally, gratefully, Gareth and the others were released due to lack of evidence.

I decided I didn't want to be detained. Or die in prison. Or throw stones at the government. I also decided that I didn't want to stay at my school any more. School was in Walmer Estate on the outskirts of the city centre, which I deemed a dangerous area, rubber bullets and Casspirs parked outside of school premises being what they were.

So I decided I was changing schools a year before I was actually supposed to.

Or at least I announced publicly that I was leaving a year early. I had seen a prospectus for a private school in a box in my mother's cupboard. I often retrieved it secretly and inhaled the pages filled with happy, neatly dressed white girls swimming and working on computers and reading or sitting in a circle on a perfectly manicured lawn with their heads thrown back, laughing. They had one coloured friend and one black friend who also laughed almost maniacally. What a happy place! The pages of the brochure were glossy and smelled of a fresh start. In that box, beneath the booklet, were shiny teal ribbons, which I assumed would be used to secure the ends of my plaits on the first day of school. I did not bother asking my parents if I was in fact changing schools. That's what I did: I gathered clues and made deductions and this would then be Reality.

I told my teacher I would be leaving at the end of the year. She was visibly disappointed and I was suitably pleased. On the final day of school, in the intense December heat from which even our little white Panama hats couldn't adequately shade us, I was called out of our long serpentine line that ran parallel to that of the other classes on the cracked tarmac and was personally congratulated and wished well by the principal.

"You will be missed, Desiree-Anne. You're off to be a small fish in a big pond," she tapped me repeatedly on the shoulder. Prophetic old bitch.

When the bell rang, heralding the endless, blissful summer holidays, I ran up the long road to my dad's awaiting sedan. As was customary, he asked to see my report. It was brilliant, as usual, but it was the folded insert that made his jaw drop rather than my usual straight As.

"Did you tell the school you're leaving?" He had swung around almost fully in the driver's seat.

"Yes," I answered, matter-of-factly, "to go to private school."

"Wait here," he commanded and climbed out of the car. I watched him make his way down the same long road I had just ascended. I knew I was in deep, deep shit.

I sat in the car, sweating, compulsively snapping the thin elastic around my chin that held my hat securely on its perch until my chin stung. A few minutes later, I saw him labour back up the road, and as he got closer to the car, I saw that the insert was now crumpled up in his fist. He got back into the driver's seat, tossed the balled paper into the back and turned the ignition.

"Why do you have to be like this?" he growled.

I slid down on the squelching vinyl backseat.

"Like what?"

"Like such a fucking liar all the time."

I did not know the answer to that question. I didn't believe I had lied intentionally. I just made up truths. Alternate realities.

CHAPTER 10

Speaking England

It was the first day of my new school, my new reality, and I had never wanted to be more white.

"Where do you live?"

"Fairways."

"Where's that?" Emma Waterford crinkled her perfect little nose. Emma's complexion was so smooth and white that it was practically transparent.

"Near Plumstead," I answered, looking down at my new brown school shoes, pressing the toes down into the perfectly manicured grass of the Lower Field.

"I think I know where that is …" she trailed. She suddenly grabbed my hand. "Come, I'll show you around."

She showed me the Lower Field, the Upper Sports Field, the tennis and netball courts. We clambered up impossibly long, narrow steps to the hall where we had assembly and which also housed a fully operational theatre. She showed me the library and the science lab, all the while rambling on about herself, her home in Constantia, her beloved Daddy and her driver, Washington, who dropped and fetched her every day.

"He's 'African'," she explained using superfluous air quotes and stated even more superfluously, "but we treat him really well and he's been with the family for years so he must be happy."

I wondered whether Washington lived with them in the posh suburb of Constantia, in a cramped bedroom at the back of the house where he polished his hard leather shoes, sitting on his small bed in his vest sleeves every night. Or whether he drove the Jaguar to the township every night to the *oohs* and *aaahs* of his jealous neighbours or whether they shamed him for working for a white family and being a sell-out to the Struggle.

I had swapped out my lime-green summer dress with the white collar for a similar pale blue one. I was now obligated to wear a royal blue blazer no matter the weather. I had a sports uniform. Springfield offered actual sport, year round. Emma had promised to show me the pool later where there was swimming and synchronised swimming for senior schoolgirls.

Everything was new and overwhelming. My clothes were new. My adored stationery was brand new. I had watched my mother wrap a cargo load of notebooks and textbooks the nights prior while sitting at the end of the glass-top dining table, eating a plum and pouring over the English setwork book.

"Next year you're doing this yourself," she warned, snipping another piece of Sellotape off the roll and adhering it to the line of sticky tape soldiers on the edge of the table. She had a system. She always had a system.

A bell clanged several times in the distance and Emma ushered me up a slope to the field where perfect little Smurfettes were falling into line according to their classes. Atop a small hill, a little brick structure housed a nun with a bullhorn: Sister Caroline, the principal. I had never met or even seen a nun before my entrance interview. This one was misshapen – I wasn't entirely sure that she had a waist or hipbones beneath her habit – and had a bespectacled, wrinkled face that broke out into an insincere, mistimed smile often (especially in the presence of parents) that showed the yellowed teeth of a Camel Filter smoker. I pondered whether she had a 40-a-day habit before giving her soul to the Holy Trinity or if she *smokkeled skyf* behind the chapel after a hard day at school.

I looked down the lines of the assembled girls. You could count the coloureds and Muslims on two hands. And the black girl on one finger. She spoke like a white child and I was later to discover that she was the daughter of a domestic worker and had been 'adopted' and raised by her mother's white employer. She even had a white brother, and they lived in Green Point.

As soon as I climbed out of the car that morning, I had decided to alter my accent too. A collection of inflections drawn from American TV shows such as *The Cosby Show*, intonations from the girls I danced with since the age of six at the University of Cape Town School of Ballet, and some manufactured brogue that saw me rolling my *rrrr*s (though I had a humiliating speech impediment that prevented me from doing this effectively and basically sounding like I came from some unchartered region of rural England). When my parents accidentally overheard me on the phone to friends or at school, they even called it "Talking England". Of course, I would drop that accent as soon as I got back in the car and by the time we pulled into the garage at home I would be speaking like exactly where I was from.

The identity crisis began enveloping me on that very first day.

My former principal had been on the money: I was now a small fish in a big pond and my psyche clambered for a way to grow bigger, swim faster.

Lies.

I chose lies.

In the years that followed I would lie pathologically about almost anything: where I lived, my family situation, how much money we had, my precocious puberty, domestic violence (though I was to discover that when I did tell the actual truth, people rarely believed me). I piled more complex lies onto more intricate fabrications. To get attention, to grow bigger, swim faster.

I did well academically until the third term when the bottle-blonde, blue-eyed Mrs Johnson called my parents in for a meeting. I thought she knew. I felt untold relief. I could stop lying now. But she had called the meeting to inform my parents that I had obtained a 'C' grade in Science and she was concerned about the sudden drop in my grades, which stood out from my streak of perfect As. My parents nodded in their concerned parental way and asked what could be done about this abhorrent situation.

"I think she needs to see a child psychologist." Mrs Jackson withdrew a piece of paper from her desk drawer and wrote the name of a therapist in her perfect handwriting. Handwriting I had already successfully managed to forge in my homework diary.

"She may," she whispered, as though I was not seated a metre away from her in a tiny front-row desk, "have adjustment issues."

More synchronised nodding from my parents, like twin metronomes.

A psychologist. I was relieved. Perhaps he or she would get it; would understand how conflicted and pained I was on a daily basis. Except, of course, in Speech and Drama on a Tuesday afternoon. That was painless and liberating. Maybe he or she would finally get it? Get me?

A psychologist though? At 10 years old. I was more than a little impressed with myself.

It was a he. He was young and cultivated a five-o'clock shadow on his baby-smooth skin to appear older. He was also wholly ineffectual. He didn't care to hear about my chronic lies or my dad's drinking or gambling, or how I felt perpetually not-good-enough. He didn't want to hear about my mom's rages, how she had smacked my thighs so hard for absentmindedly forgetting my shoes at school the term before. Or the time in Standard 2 when she hit me on the back of my legs with a wooden spoon. This was a deviation from her norm, because she preferred using her bare hands, or my father's. My Standard 2 teacher had ratted me out for cutting up some of my old clothes to create costumes for the play I was writing and directing during breaks. It was a suspense-thriller-comedy; it was also the last play I ever wrote. The pain of wood on thighs and the inability to sit at the dinner table without the pillow my brother brought me ensured the end of my career as a playwright.

No one laid a hand on my brother – not that he ever got into any trouble – because of the fear of him seizing. No one ever touched him. Not like they did me. No, what Junior Psychologist was most interested in was the C grade and how to pull me out of the doldrums of academia. I spent the rest of three boring sessions lying and placating him too. He seemed very self-satisfied. I let him. There was clearly a system at play here and I had cracked the code wide open. He called for a family session with all in attendance. My parents appeared nervous. My brother appeared completely disenchanted. I turned on the waterworks. My dad offered to leave the room with me and, as we paced the halls, me still sobbing, he asked, "Baby, what is it you want?" I forced out the last wail and – as rehearsed – blurted out, "I just want us to tell each other that we love each other more!" That should shut them up.

It did. We returned to the over air-conditioned, sterile room and my father announced my emotional request. Everyone seemed relieved and self-congratulatory, especially Junior Psych. I thought everyone would burst into a round of rousing applause. He had fixed me. How awesome to be him. We agreed that we would Declare Our Love for each other ad nauseam. Which happened for a while, awkwardly at the end of phone calls, at bedtime, randomly in passing. My brother did not buy into it, but I was okay with his exclusion because I felt he was loved enough anyway.

It all lasted about three months and then the loving platitudes wore off. The drinking, gambling and raging continued unabated.

Only four weeks before I pulled my Science grade back up to an A aggregate. Only 30 more years of intermittent psychotherapy before I finally got honest.

CHAPTER 11

The Truth in the Lie

The lies continued. But when I saw an advert in a newspaper for open auditions at the Waterfront Theatre School they skyrocketed to a whole new level. Because now the lies could be dignified as 'acting'. I was 13 years old.

"You'll need two prepared soliloquys, one Shakespearean and one contemporary," the clear, crisp voice on the other end of the phone said. "Auditions are next Saturday. Do you know where we are located?"

"Of course," I lied and hung up. I frantically looked the word 'soliloquy' up in the dictionary. I spent every conceivable free moment behind my closed bedroom door rehearsing Ophelia from the 'mad scene' in *Hamlet*, as well as a monologue from my favourite childhood book, *Alice in Wonderland*. I had no idea how I was going to get to the school by 1 pm on Saturday or where it was, but I was going to do it. Saturday morning rolled around and I thought I'd puke from anxiety. As the big and little hands travelled around the face of the clock on the mantelpiece and edged towards noon, I sat in my room, on the edge of the bed, crying, already dressed in my red-and-black bell-sleeve dress and opaque tights and Docs, hair scraped back in a bun and held in place with extra-strength gel I had found in the depths of the bathroom cupboard.

My cousin Mark came in and asked what the problem was. I

blurted it all out and showed him the clipping from the 'Tonight' section of *The Argus*.

"I'll take you," he said.

I hugged him, thanked him, and we raced to the Victoria & Alfred Waterfront. The Waterfront Theatre School was not actually in the Waterfront, we soon found out. We eventually located it just near the entrance to the working harbour. I jumped out the car at 1.15 pm and ran into the pale blue building and straight into a young man doing countless pirouettes down the hall.

"I'm here to audition," I explained. He pointed down the hall, not breaking his perfect, leaping twirls. The place smelled old and dusty, noise emanating from every corner: shouting, musical instruments completely out of synch with one another, repetitive knocking that had to be tap-dancing. I was in heaven.

I found the office. I found the owner, Delia Sainsbury. I had seen her on TV and was awe-struck.

"You're late," she heeded. "And as artists we have to be punctual. Why do you want to be a student here?"

"Because I can't not," the words tumbled effortlessly from my lips. "I have to act. It's the only thing that makes me happy."

She seemed satisfied and made me fill in another form, though my mind went blank frequently and my hands were shaking. Several students entered and exited the office while I sat there; they seemed so confident, so beautiful, and so happy. I had to be one of them.

I was ushered down the passage into a small studio space where I performed my two prepared pieces – Ophelia and Alice – to an audience of one, a young teacher called Miranda. Afterwards, as she scribbled on a clipboard, I alternated placing the toes of one foot on the other, and biting my lip.

Miranda cleared her throat and looked up from her notes and spoke. Her voice was like honey dripping straight from the comb. "That was great, really good. Have you acted before?"

"Only at Speech and Drama at school," I replied.

"The only critique I would offer is, at the end, don't look to the audience for approval. Both times you looked to me to see if you had done well. Rather just hold a pose. And next time, wear all black. Those sleeves interfere with your performance and the colour is distracting."

I was mortified. Had I failed?

But Miranda continued … "Do you sing?"

I shook my head, embarrassed. I was utterly tone deaf.

"Hmm …" More frantic scribbling. "Do you dance?"

"Yes."

"Two out of three isn't bad. Follow me."

We exited the studio and made our way back to Delia's office. Like the others, she didn't knock, but simply marched in and demanded the others leave. She placed the clipboard on the desk in front of Delia and I saw an A circled a few times at the top of the page.

Delia scooped up the clipboard and scanned the contents of the page.

"Well, Desiree-Anne," she started. No one ever used my full name unless I was in big shit. "It appears you're a very talented young lady. You definitely have what it takes to join us here at the theatre school."

My heart began to race. I thought I might faint.

"How old are you?"

"Thirteen."

"You're going to have to give these to your parents," and she handed me a pile of forms, "and see what they say, but we would love to have you here as a student."

"Thank you so much!" I responded over-effusively. I wanted to fall down at her feet and kiss her black ballet pumps. "I want to, I will …" I was stammering, teeth chattering. I clutched the forms to my chest, "I will be back. Thank you, Ms Sainsbury!"

I half-ran down the hall and out of the building until I reached Mark's car, pulled opened the passenger door and sank into the blistering leather seat.

"So?"

"I did it. I got in!"

So it was that drama became my life. I attended classes twice a week, three times if you counted the extramural at school; it was the highlight of my little realm. I took to wearing black all the time, not just for auditions. I inhaled scripts; I practised furiously even when I didn't need to. At the end of my second year, I received the trophy for The Royal Academy Student of the Year. I was the best in *the entire college.*

I could act exceptionally well and I did, especially in my everyday life. I slipped in and out of my own manufactured roles. When meeting strangers, I often pretended to be a foreigner, deftly transitioning from my own accent to American or French or Italian. I favoured being American because I felt it was more likely that a dark-skinned foreign-exchange student would come from there than from Paris or Rome. You had to keep it believable. The living lie had to be sustained and credible. The surrealism of acting began to merge with and bleed into my own life as I gained the ability to instantly morph myself into a cast of finely crafted characters. I could be the miserable and misunderstood Goth, the happy hippie chick, the angst-riddled intellectual, the bad girl, and my most prized and accomplished role, the good girl.

I was a trained professional. By the age of 15, I could be whatever you wanted me to be.

CHAPTER 12

Murder Most Foul

I liked the control that being a professional chameleon brought with it. I did not like surprises. Like when my Ma Eileen passed or when I acquired a new older brother and then, in my teens, a new younger brother and found out that my father was a serial cheater. Or that time my older cousin and his girlfriend thought it entertaining to drop me at the gates of Grassy Park cemetery late one night and drive away. They came back a few terrifying, traumatic minutes later, laughing about the ingenuity and hilarity of their practical joke. I have never set foot in a graveyard since.

Because the adults around me were so secretive and closeted, I quickly developed astounding skills of detection. I was constantly looking for and analysing clues left carelessly, combining assumption and logic, often leading to intricate hypotheses. My deductive reasoning was invariably correct so I usually saw things coming a mile away even from a tender age. *I knew it*, I would think, *I just knew it*. Then be instantly saddened by the truth I had uncovered or had eventually revealed itself. Even though we never talked about anything, ever, the truth had a tendency to force itself out from the shadows like stinking pus from an infected wound.

I would demand, *need*, to know everything. I always asked questions. I was hyper vigilant. It was my way of keeping myself safe, staying in control, managing the ever-present terror of both the known and unknown that gave me childhood stomach ailments and chest infections, and crippling insomnia in adolescence. I took to staying awake alone. Reading entire books, rehearsing imaginary scenes about my fantastical future with Keanu Reeves, tiptoeing into the kitchen to steal food, pacing up and down the dark passage, watching late-night television in the lounge with the sound so low that my nose was practically pressed to the screen, or standing at the foot of my parents' bed while they slept, daring to take the chance to crawl in between their turned backs or will them to wake up to comfort me – neither of which happened, of course.

Or I'd talk to the dogs, pavement specials Fluffy and Chico. We'd inherited them when my parents bought the house. They'd initially been re-homed to family of their original owners, somewhere in the northern suburbs, Bellville, but a few weeks after we took occupation, we found them waiting, expectantly, at the front door. Somehow, they had found their way back home and, after much pleading on my part, they stayed.

I was allergic to all animals, feather or fur, but I loved them – especially Fluffy – so I sacrificed myself to the allergy gods in exchange for unconditional doggy adoration.

Then one day, when I was 14, my father entered my room and stood motionless.

"I have something to tell you, Dezzy."

I was preoccupied with three different things simultaneously – none of which was homework, ever. Homework was done before school in the morning, obviously.

"What is it?" I didn't look up but detected a new, unfamiliar tone in my father's voice. I would later recognise it as guilt.

He couldn't bring himself to say it, spit out the words, but when I looked up at him I knew, *I just knew*. By the time he managed to spill those dreadful words – "I had Fluffy put to sleep ..." – I was halfway down the passage and on the front stoep, screaming Fluffy's name, crying and searching, the kennel, the back yard. I ran back to the stoep where my dad stood.

"It had to be done. He was old."

"He wasn't sick though!" I screamed, falling to my knees on the hard slate tiles.

"He was becoming difficult to look after," he continued, softly.

"You *killed* him! *You killed my dog!*"

My head reeled with confusion and that familiar rage of injustice. I felt sick. I felt out of control. I was hysterical and my father knew better than to step on that train track. I stayed slumped on the floor, sobbing and dry heaving, vomit threatening to lurch up out of my mouth at any moment. And then, I stopped. I went quiet and everything about me, the world, went cold. I gathered my shattered self up from the floor and walked past my father.

"You killed my dog," I whispered, hoarsely.

I didn't eat or speak to anyone for days. I didn't shed another tear. I had gone numb from the brutal betrayal and silent from the searing hatred.

I vowed there would be No More Surprises.

PART 2

Breaking the Rules

CHAPTER 13

Silent Night

The man to my left extended his hand in greeting. He coupled it with an earnest, overly zealous smile that made me want to vomit on his shiny shoes and punch him in his stupid mouth, with the tight fist I had formed in the pocket of my jacket.

"Peace be with you," he offered. I turned my entire body away from his insipid greeting only to meet my father's own skew fingers offering the same saccharine blessing.

"Fuck you," I hissed, inaudibly, and buried my hands deeper into the jacket. The pungent incense singed my nose and burned my throat. I felt suffocated. I could not wait for this hellish church service to be over.

I had stopped attending church exactly one week after I had been confirmed at age 14. I had not wanted to be confirmed in the first place but my parents had felt it the Right Thing To Do and I had been dragged involuntarily to church every Sunday and confirmation classes every Wednesday afternoon to ensure my passage to Heaven. Followed by cream doughnuts from Coimbra by way of some kind of reward. No one had bothered asking me if I believed in Heaven – or God for that matter – or whether Paradise was in fact my intended final destination.

It hadn't always been that way. From the time I was 10 years old, my parents had sent me to Scripture Union camps for a week in the summer holidays. I loved camp. I loved how they unveiled another, hipper version of Jesus and played obstacle courses and had bonfires with roasted marshmallows. So every year, without fail, I would give my life to this Jesus of the Summer Camp. One year, I told my dad when I returned and he burst into tears, which I neither understood nor cared to. Seeing my father cry was enough to halt all further enquiries. But it only took a few weeks post-camp for my relationship with Jesus to wane. It's hard to be enthusiastic about anyone when there are no gooey marshmallows involved.

I knew the Anglican Church thing was an elaborate scam. Not quite as much as the Catholic dogma that I was force fed at convent school, but the bullshit doctrine of the Church of England was firmly established when I had been asked to participate in the rite of confession towards the end of the pre-confirmation process. I had lied through my braced teeth – omitting tales of premarital sexual lewdness and petty theft and devastating dishonesty – and had been more than pleasantly surprised when I had not spontaneously combusted within the wooden walls of the confessional.

God had not seen me; He clearly neither knew nor cared.

So I made a unilateral decision to no longer follow the pastoral flock. A decision my parents did not seem to mind now that their parental and moral duties had been performed – until that Christmas Eve, until that Midnight Mass. It had been an unspoken non-issue the entire day until about 8 pm.

"Get dressed for church," my mother stopped in at my doorway. She was expertly inserting her diamond stud into her left earlobe. I lay stretched out on my bed, listening to *The Stone Roses* on my Walkman.

I slid my orange foam headphones off my ears and onto my shoulders. "I'm not going."

"Yes, you are. Get dressed." She did a 90-degree turn and walked off to her own bedroom in a suffocating cloud of Dior Poison.

My mother's words held such cutting finality that they made me sit upright and swear out loud. I untangled myself from the straps of my Walkman and cords of my headphones. I slowly peeled off my clothes and – standing in my mismatched underwear and stretched socks – surveyed the contents of my cupboard. Though primarily black, my clothes were a loud and confusing mixture of various eclectic influences: teenage rebel, Goth, punk and distorted body image. My style – and one would have to use that term rather loosely – clashed heavily with my mother's last nerve. When I appeared in any given doorway, my appearance always elicited a disapproving cluck of the tongue, a disparaging look or sigh heavy with passive-aggression. I had learned how to ward these critical expressions off with a well-rehearsed and heavily fortified armour of adolescent apathy. My mother took my dress sense so personally, as though I was intentionally trying to embarrass her or the family. The truth was that I loathed my body and had no clue how to clothe it appropriately or how to externally adorn what was happening internally. Hence, I always looked like a bit of a fucked-up mess; because that was my emotional reality.

When my body changed, I had been wholly unprepared. I started developing breasts and pubic hair at the age of 11. I stole my father's Schick razor and carefully tried to remove all hairy evidence of invasive womanhood. Not having an open relationship with my mother, I did not have anyone with whom to discuss these things. She never had The Talk with me so I remained scared and ill informed. I had to get my first bra by writing about it in my 'Secret Diary' and leaving it in the hiding place where I knew my mother would find it and religiously read it. When I got my period a few years later, I truly thought I was bleeding as a direct result of a punishment for masturbating – as my mother had so ominously predicted. During this time I was cursed with raging, weeping eczema across most of my body; I hated my hair, which was *kroes* and crazy and not straight and silky like the pretty white girls; I wore braces on my protruding Bugs-Bunny teeth for four years; and I was the shortest person that I knew – and I knew some 10-year-olds. In Standard 4, a girl at school said that if you didn't have a gap between your thighs you were fat. I never had a thigh gap, so I thought I was fat from the time I was 12 until, well, forever.

For Mass I chose an oversized monochrome shirt that buttoned down from the neck to the knee and a black knee-length skirt. I considered wearing my 12 lace-up Doc Martens – the ones with the blue and green satin ribbons where shoelaces should have been – but thought they may be a tad disrespectful on Jesus's birthday so slipped my pantyhosed feet into more acceptable shoes and examined myself in the mirror, the edges of which were decorated with dried, very dead rose buds and carefully cut-out pictures of Keanu Reeves. Acceptable, surely? I *really* did not want to piss my mother off on Christmas Eve.

I scraped my hair back in a bushy ponytail and didn't even bother to try to smooth down the wisps of hair that puffed up defiantly at my hairline. At the last minute, I grabbed my prized hooded, camouflage jacket that I had bought at Sergeant Pepper's off Greenmarket Square. I had saved up for months to buy it and wore it all the time, even in the muggy December heat. I paused at the door, turned, and then threw the jacket back on the bed.

Leave the jacket. Just leave the jacket. She hates the jacket.

I walked down the passage to the lounge. My mother sat on the couch smoking one of her Courtleigh Slims, dressed in an emerald-green jersey-knit dress with three-quarter-length sleeves and that came down to a modest length past her knees. The dress was cinched in at the waist with a glossy black patent-leather belt accentuating my mother's shapely figure. She wore black patent-leather heels, one of which was now tapping impatiently on the carpeted floor. My brother sat on the opposite end of the couch, slouched over a game of Donkey Kong on his handheld console. My father had just poured a drink at the foldout bar attached to the cream melamine TV stand.

"What are you wearing?"

My heart plummeted in my chest. "Clothes."

Wrong answer.

"I'm dressed for church."

"No, you're not," she barked. "Go get changed."

"This is what I'm wearing. I don't have anything else … and I look fine."

My mother shot a look at my father who, like an Olympic

athlete in a relay race, passed the facial expression expertly like a non-verbal baton onto me.

"Your mother told you to go get changed."

"I told you—"

Pain splintered across my middle back as it connected with the wall. My father, his hands on my shoulders, had shoved me almost across the room. My head snapped forward and as it did, he dug his fingers into the base of my ponytail and twisted it, forcing my entire head and body to turn. I instinctively wrapped my hands around his hand and tried to pry my hair loose. My scalp felt as though it might tear right off.

"Why don't you fucking listen?" he shouted breathlessly.

I couldn't see his face. He had my long ponytail slung over his shoulder and was drag-pulling me down the passage. I scraped my knuckles across the bumpy wall trying to grab onto something, to make it stop, and eventually hooked my fingers around the frame of my bedroom door. As I did, my father swung me around by my hair and into the door of the cupboard. I held out my hands to lessen the impact but was too slow and hit my forehead. I ricocheted off the cupboard door and landed on my back on the floor. I lay there, stunned, feeling as though there were no longer any bones in my body.

"Find something decent to wear. We'll wait in the car."

Later, as I stood at the end of the cramped pew in that smoky church, awkwardly playing my involuntarily assigned role in the Christmas Eve episode of *Happy Families*, I – clad in an ill-fitting floral-paisley dress, a navy linen jacket bought only because it had looked black in the shop and black pumps that were one size too small – was quietly outraged by the overbearing hypocrisy of so very many things all at once.

The church bells in the distance gonged and chimed midnight, heralding in the joyous Noël.

I wanted to scream.

Fuck Christmas. Fuck Everything.

CHAPTER 14

The Papers

After that night I became even more silently angry and openly apathetic about almost everything. I wore my "I don't give a fuck attitude" as often as I wore my camo jacket. I was especially angry with my mother. She listened in on my telephone conversations with friends, she still read my diary. I couldn't speak to anyone about how I was feeling, filled with suppressed rage and mind-numbing confusion. So I adopted the approach of not talking much at all.

One evening when I was 15, I sat hunched over on the couch. I was ready to go to a music concert with my friend, but my mother had called me into the lounge to tell me Something Important.

She shoved some papers into my hands.

"There," she barked. "Read them!"

I lifted the first yellowed sheet up slowly, unwillingly, but she snatched it from my trembling hands as the rest fell onto my lap.

"I'll tell you what they say." This was clearly not going to be a conversation.

"Okay."

"They say, 'Application for Divorce'. And do you see this ...?" She stabbed her index finger repeatedly at the offending paragraph.

"No."

"This!" She lowered the page down to my eye level and the tip of her fingernail underlined a date: 1977.

"You were one year old. I wanted to divorce him then already."

She inhaled deeply through her nostrils in an effort to maintain some semblance of composure. Her chest rose and fell and rose and fell again before she was ready to continue.

"Ask me," she challenged me. "Ask me why I didn't?"

It was a rhetorical question obviously. I knew the answer, but I felt caged, with no escape. I felt obliged to participate in this horrendous reveal.

"Why didn't you?"

"Because of you," she leaned in close enough for me to smell the smoke on her breath. "Because of you children!" More of an accusation than an expression of consideration and love.

You really shouldn't have bothered is what I wanted to say, but I didn't. Instead I said, "Thank you," and motioned to get up from the couch and leave the room. I was tired of perpetually listening to her complain about my father and vice versa. I had become accustomed to this behind-the-back bullshit, but I was worn out by their refusal to talk to each other and instead use me as an involuntary sounding board for their ongoing and draining marital gripes.

"I'm not done yet." She lit her third cigarette and rifled through the papers again, cigarette expertly held between the crook of her index and middle finger. My mother could smoke while doing pretty much anything: working, cooking, destroying someone's life. "There is something else I have to tell you."

I sat back down.

"You may think I'm the bad guy." Her demeanour was less aggressive, more long-suffering martyr. It was a tone I was exceedingly familiar with. "You take all your *kak* teenage moods out on *me*. You fight with *me* all the time. And you worship him and think he can do no wrong, but let me tell you something ..." She pushed another page into my hands. "Those are receipts ..." she paused. "Receipts of payments made to the mother of your brother."

I looked up at her, deeply confused. "I only have one brother?"

Two, at most, I thought. Brendon, from my father's first failed marriage, and Alcid-John, my *real* brother.

She sat down next to me, sinking into the side of the couch with the broken spring. "No," she said, almost emphatically. "You have another brother that your father had with another woman when you were a year old. He was cheating on me while you were still a baby." She struggled to hide the disgust and pain of the memory in her voice. "Your brother should be 16 now."

I felt instantly nauseous and wanted to vomit. I was 15. Instead I cried, I sobbed.

Everything I thought I knew about my father was a lie.

"I'm only telling you this for your own good," she continued, ignoring my meltdown. "Because I heard he may be going to your drama school. He is apparently an excellent dancer. I didn't want you to meet him and suddenly figure out that you had the same father. His name is Lee-Jason, in case you do meet him. He does know about you, as far as I know."

That scenario flashed in my frazzled mind. Seeing him, seeing my father's eyes or nose or charming smile or curly hair, seeing the intrinsically familiar. I played through the dialogue that would follow:

"Hi, don't I know you?"

"I think I know you too …"

"You really do look like someone I know. I just can't place it now …"

"Your father. I look like your father. My father."

Jesus Christ, no.

"Can I go now?" I had heard my father's car pull up in the driveway and I was already standing at the door to the lounge.

She sank into the La-Z-Boy, exhausted and disappointed, as though this was not the outcome she had expected. She was more accustomed to my raging histrionics than bitter tears. Perhaps she had wanted me to become hysterical and confront my father myself. Relieve her pain, create my own.

I ran out to the car, climbed into the passenger's seat, and my father and I drove in silence to my friend Casey's house. I wanted to tell him I knew. I wanted to ask if he knew that she'd told me. I had so many questions. I idolised this man, even with his undeniable frailties. Even though he'd smashed me against a wall. We were so much alike, from our curly hair down to our crooked fingers, from our dark sense of humour to our silly playfulness. He got me more than anyone else. I looked over at him, driving with one hand on the steering wheel as he always did, and saw the same man, but now my father was also a cheating fraud with a bastard child.

I had another brother. My head was spinning. The words lay restlessly on my lips but the burning rage kept me from uttering them. I was angry with him, yes, but even more enraged with my mother for smearing putrid shit all over my idea of and deep love for my father. I wanted to ask him so many things. I needed him to make sense of this intolerable pain I felt. I needed him to make everything okay again.

But I didn't. Ever. I never spoke to my father about his other child. It was just one of the Things We Never Spoke About. Ever.

I only met Lee-Jason and his mom at a Narcotics Anonymous meeting in Grassy Park 12 years later.

My mother's disclosure meant that, at the very least, I didn't end up unwittingly fucking my brother after an NA meeting.

After my mother dished the dirt on my father, I leapt at any excuse to get out of the house. The Fringe became my haven.

My father would drop me off on a Friday or Saturday night and reluctantly collect me again at 1 am or thereabouts – 'thereabouts' being the time I finally made my way to him waiting in the car outside because I had conveniently forgotten the time.

I loved that club. I felt so at home there among the other misfits and rejects, orphans and atheists. In the beginning I never drank alcohol, I never touched a drug. I would venture down the metal fire-escape staircase to The Pit where everyone smoked weed. Everyone but me. I didn't feel the need to. Yet. I came to the smoky club to perve on the pseudo-Goth guys or dance awkwardly to Nine Inch Nails or the B52s or REM on the sticky dance floor. I loved that I became recognised as a regular and that the DJ always knew exactly what songs I would be requesting as I stood patiently on tiptoes at the booth. Belonging was so important to me.

It was 1994, and it was going to be a big year for the entire country politically but also a big year for me. I would soon be starting at Abbotts College, a small Standard 10-only college that focused purely on academics. I had been expelled – no, asked to leave – Springfield Convent for pinning a small, folded red ribbon on my blazer in support of Aids awareness. One of the identical Harvey twins – Tasha or Lisa, I could never distinguish between them – was a prefect and demanded that I remove it. I refused. I was marched off to the office of the principal, Sister Pia, and a conversation laden with ignorance, fear and prejudice ensued. I could have sworn that by the time we concluded our discussion, I was given permission to continue wearing the satiny ribbon. I was wrong. Or they were hypocrites, which was the more likely scenario. When I proudly displayed the ribbon at after-break assembly the next day, one of those interfering twins sent me back up to the office, to the penguin-shaped principal.

"But you said I could wear it," I protested, rubbing my shoe up and down my mid-calf, eczema flaring up as we spoke.

"I said no such thing," the Penguin retorted. "I think we need to call a meeting with your parents." And I was duly dismissed, unpinning the ribbon as I walked out of the reception area and feeling utterly betrayed and confused.

The Meeting ensued. It took less than 10 minutes. The Penguin, the vice-principal Mrs Brice and my father attended. He had been wanting me to attend Abbotts, where my brother had excelled a year before, anyway. I had flatly refused. But now it sounded like I had little choice. We were, however, faced with a new dilemma. Private schools like Springfield do not expel learners; they were "invited" to leave as though it was their own idea.

"Does she have to leave now?" my father asked. It was mid-way through the second term.

"No, no," Mrs Brice answered. "She can see out the year."

Thanks a fuckload, I thought. Utter humiliation for a whole two and a half more terms. My father was elated. I was absolutely gutted. I did not like change even if I hated the place where I was. Until it actually came time to move schools, then everything started shifting.

A week or so before matric began I was already making friends with fellow learners at the college who also hung out at The Fringe. And friends with their friends. Like Jacob Schneider. I was absolutely besotted with him. I wanted to speak to him but was paralysed with anxiety, debilitated by my innate shyness. So I drank almost half a bottle of cheap and nasty Tassies. It drips with cliché, I know, but I truly felt like I had come home.

When I had drunk alcohol for the first time on Christmas Day at Auntie Sybil's house when I was 13 – a few too many glasses of saccharine sweet JC Le Roux sparkling wine – I did not love it. I ended up in tears. *Dronk verdriet*, they call it. I planted myself in front of the television to watch a made-for-TV movie that featured the love of my fantastical life, Keanu Reeves. I've subsequently learned that fanaticism and obsession are core traits of addicts. I was both.

I was utterly entranced by Keanu's trademark wooden performance when my Uncle Edward switched the electricity off at the mains, rendering the screen blank and taking my beloved Keanu away from me into the darkness of the television. I burst into tears and wailed insufferably. The adults laughed at my intoxicated misery.

Drunks ugly cry. I never ever cried when I was drunk after that.

That night with Jacob, though, trying desperately to catch his attention, the wine set fire to my cerebral cortex. My conversation was fluid and witty. I felt sexy, desirable and unashamedly aroused. My self-consciousness faded into the noisy background music of the dodgy tavern.

Alcohol. Suddenly, it all made such perfect sense. I truly was my father's daughter.

CHAPTER 15

Toothbrush Tricks

Now that the divorce papers had been thrown on the table, it was inevitable that the deterioration in my parents' relationship would find a home in me. Within a few weeks of finding myself on the cramped campus of Abbotts College in my final year of school, self-consciousness and self-loathing hit me like an anvil.

There were boys – unlike Springfield, my previous bitchy all-girl convent school. While my former school provided safety in terms of vanity – you didn't have to worry about the zit on your nose or food stuck in your braces or your fuzzy underarm hair during swimming practice or on your legs throughout winter – at Springfield you could be ousted from a clique on a weekly basis without so much as written notice just for doing sweet fuck all. You could also be teased – they call it 'bullying' now – for having weeping, scabby eczema on your legs, or even for being too pretty or excelling at school work.

So although I had changed schools, nothing about me had changed intrinsically or extrinsically. Although my orthodontic braces had been removed the year before and my smile was nothing short of killer, I still struggled with eczema and its accompanying scars, with my confrontational hair, and I was still short as shit with no sign of the elusive, desirable thigh gap.

I was in no way prepared for the heady hormonal surge that

came with attending a co-ed school, one where you could wear casual clothes. I could hardly dress myself on weekends, and now I was forced to choose clothes that made me look semi-attractive every day of the week.

I only learned the word 'dysmorphia' much later on in life – a condition in which someone falsely believes that there is something seriously wrong with his or her appearance. I had that in bucket loads. And I had strong encouragement in forming these beliefs: friends had told me that my hair was "funny and weird" and that one should have two eyebrows, not just one, as I did. That was before I started shaving off, with surgical precision, the fine hairs that joined the thicker two brows. My dad – innocently, I believe, when he had had a few too many one day – pulled me onto his lap and called me his "fat little baby girl". My mother often commented about the unappealing size of my bum. So when I looked in the mirror I saw pure ugly, a sin against nature. My reflection screamed, "Fat pig!" I saw rolls of excess flesh, too-large breasts, dimpled cellulite. I truly believed that if I were thinner, life would be better. In fact I deeply believed that if I was different, everything would be better.

But my unacceptably fat body was a good place to start.

I scanned the rotating metal shelf at the pharmacy off Greenmarket Square. I didn't know which one to choose so I decided on the name brand that spoke straight to my intended goal: Thinz. I took a brown-beige box off the shelf and nervously approached the counter to pay as though I was actually buying drugs. I imagined that the content *norpseudoephedrine hydrochloride* listed on the back of the box could not be entirely good for you.

I sensed the cashier was judging me as she scanned my borderline-obese body, my rolls of stomach fat not hidden all that well under my uniform baggy, long-sleeved top, the flabbiness of my short thighs. She was probably thinking – as some people even went so far as to verbalise – "You'd be so pretty if you were thin."

She took my money, apparently approving of my course of action, and I made my escape out of the cramped pharmacy and into the light and noise of the cobbled square. The box of pills was safely stashed in my backpack, but I wanted them in my body now, melting fat cells instantaneously.

I had one hour to get to drama class. I barricaded myself in a dingy public toilet stall that never locked, like the rest, and never had toilet paper, like the rest. I perched on the toilet seat and retrieved the slimming tablets from my bag. I tore open the box and slid out the blister pack, removing one tablet. It was translucent, minuscule beads of magical medication stored within. I put one in my mouth, then two, then three. I exited the stall, leaned over the stained washbasin and drank water from the tap. I felt immediately more slender, like the curved-hip lady conservatively covering her breasts on the box.

An hour later, as I was running through my vocal warm-up exercises at the Waterfront Theatre School, my tongue became inconveniently disobedient and numb. Then the tremors started, all over my body; my stomach felt as though it had caved in on itself and I wanted to vomit. I could feel that my eyes had widened like saucers and I wanted to run across the hall and also collapse on the stage at the same time.

And I had no desire to eat.

I would definitely be doing this again.

Which I did, daily, at home and at school. I spent all my money on Thinz and my original anxiety about purchasing them turned quite cavalier. I pharmacy-hopped to avoid questioning and more judgement. Over weeks, months, my tolerance increased and I was ingesting six to eight pills every day, sometimes twice a day. I became comfortable with the side effects. In fact, they made me feel powerful, like I had super-human attributes. "Look at me! I don't need food like the other humans do!" my growling, snarling stomach screamed quietly. I had no appetite at all and the weight began to shift and fall off. My food began to speak to me.

"Don't eat me," the chips would say. "You're doing so well. I'll just undo all your good work and make you fat again."

So when I did eat or was forced to in public – I had taken to 'eating' in my bedroom and feeding my supper to the dogs and giving away my lunch to hungry fellow learners at school or throwing it in the Charity Box after break – I purged.

I didn't take well to sticking my fingers down my throat. My digits were too short to activate any spectacular vomiting. I would just gag and spit would run stupidly down my chin. So I used my toothbrush, holding it in one hand while the other rested on the toilet bowl, sliding the handle back over my tongue and a bit further until the end slid past my nonexistent tonsils. Dry heaving followed. I slid it in a little further and then … purging paradise. My last meal would lurch forward from the depths of my digestive system and land in the water made florid blue by the Toilet Duck. And no matter what I had or had not consumed, there were *always* pieces of undigested carrot in my puke.

I carried my toothbrush wherever I went and vomited after every shameful mouthful. I would then brush my teeth to hide the acrid smell and bitter taste of bile. My toothbrush bristles became worn and ineffectual but I would not replace it. It was my Excalibur. Priceless and powerful.

Within a year, the combination of purging and Thinz saw me drop from a podgy size 14 to a slim 8. I attracted a lot more attention from the opposite sex, but still I felt neither desirable nor beautiful. In fact, I felt morbidly obese and still hid my rapidly diminishing frame under oversized clothes.

I needed to be thinner still. They were all right: I *would* be so pretty if I was thinner. And I knew that unless I was thin enough, I was never going to get naked in front of anyone and lose my cherry.

CHAPTER 16

Not the Same Any More

I never imagined that I would lose my virginity in an orgy.

I had preserved my Vestal Virgin status like a guard watching over a Japanese prisoner-of-war. I wasn't exactly frigid; I was just terrified of sex, even if it was consensual. Especially if it was consensual. I was petrified of that level of intimacy. And I was especially afraid of getting naked in front of a boy if I was fat. By the time I started dating my first boyfriend, Lucas, I had dropped down to a size 10. But when I slept over at his mother's house, I shared the bed with him fully clothed and issued dire warnings about him "not trying his luck". I prized my chastity and was on a mission to achieve that all-important gap between my thighs. It was also extremely important to me that I *chose* to whom I lost my cherry.

So no one was more surprised than me to find myself splayed out on one side of the double bed, like an amputated starfish, naked, one forearm covering my ample breasts and disturbingly erect nipples. In a room full of people.

"Move over. You're hurting her. You're not doing it right."

Craig acquiesced and took his place as avid spectator alongside

Shaun and Lucas, my ex.

They were watching, fascinated and aroused, as Hazel slid her lithe, milky frame down my own, positioned herself between my open legs and commenced to lick and suck expertly at my excited vagina. There was nothing about her slow, languid licks and sucks that made me either uncomfortable or need to fake the impending orgasm. I lay back with eyes closed and my body writhing slowly as she expertly stripped away all of my feminine fears and led me to unholy ecstasy. I could not tell if she was precariously balancing the roles of exhibitionist or lover but, in that moment, I did not care.

All I could think was, "I'm losing my virginity to a woman." And the thought did not displease me.

It had started so suddenly. I had been sitting on a corduroy beanbag in the lounge, pushing my ass deeper into its folds to get more comfortable. But now I couldn't reach the drinking glass half-filled with red wine that was resting on the small side table. Maybe I could ask that freckle-faced, ginger-haired boy on the couch to pass it to me? Except his hands were too busy cupping the small breasts of the lanky girl from the German high school. I'd hate to interrupt that fumbling sexual exchange. So I pushed myself up out of the beanbag, onto my knees, scooped the glass up by its stem, and then settled back into my corduroy haven.

More comfortable. Still bored. Not drunk enough.

As I sipped on my wine, Hazel and Marion appeared almost mystically in the space where the coffee table used to be. They were dancing, together, intimately and seductively to the Edith Piaf record spinning on Lucas's mother's old turntable. I watched them, half embarrassed, fully fascinated, as they swooped and gyrated and moulded their bodies into one another. As the last strains of 'La Vie en Rose' breathed off the scratchy record, they bolted out of the lounge, leaving most of the room's inhabitants both confused and aroused.

I took another large gulp of my wine. Marion appeared, kneeling in front of me.

"Come with me." It wasn't so much a request as a demand and I complied.

Hand in hand, we entered Lucas's room. Shaun and Craig were seated on the bed, eyes shining from liquor and the ostensible promise of sex.

"I've always wanted to know," ventured Shaun, "how do you kiss?"

Up until a few weeks ago, his younger brother had been the only one I locked lips with. Not the first boy; there had been Lorenzo Johnson on the bus ride back from Scripture Union camp, him 17 and me 13. I had only kissed him because I had solemnly vowed to kiss a boy, any boy, before camp was over and I saw the journey home from Port Elizabeth as my last shot. There had subsequently been one or two making-out sessions, but with boys I had very little interest in. But I loved kissing. I loved the way a good kisser could make your toes curl in your sand shoes or make you gasp through already heavy breathing. I loved to have my tongue licked and my lips gently bitten. I soon discovered that not many adolescent boys possessed these skills. Instead, my dalliances were awkward and involved clashing braces and far too much dribbling saliva.

Lucas, however, was a great kisser. We had met in that last year of high school and had actually dated for three and a half whole weeks. He had written me a seven-page letter that was a heady, scrawled mixture of current affairs and emotional cravings. I ended the relationship outside Bob's Bistro – the same place where we shared our first sweet, sensual kiss – because he made me "too happy".

That was the start of a life-long pattern: *I'm going to hurt you before you even think of hurting me.*

"I've also wanted to know," added Craig, leaning back on the single unmade bed.

"Okay," I replied, squarely facing Shaun, my body bubbling and my mind racing, "I'll show you."

I perched on the bed and leaned in, locking lips with Shaun as though I were a finalist in a kissing contest. I slid my tongue around his mouth, which tasted of red wine and sweet pseudo-intellect, and then pulled back, awaiting my appraisal.

He licked his bottom lip. "You taste so sweet," he announced, turning to Craig. "You should really try that."

Craig turned to me and cupped the back of my head in his hand, eagerly pulling my lips towards him. We kissed. He, too, was pleased. Lucas stood at the edge of the bed watching his ex-girlfriend lock lips with his brother and his friend, somewhat amused, somewhat despondent.

As though I had passed some unspoken test, Marion and Hazel ran into the room and each grabbed a hand, hurriedly ushering me into Mrs Breen's bedroom. I knew what was about to take place. The puritan virgin was going to take part in an orgy.

Five semi-clad or entirely naked people. There was much fumbling and groping and exchanging of saliva. Lucas sat in the corner in an armchair, a visible voyeur, until he was called to participate. I was relieved. We had broken up a few weeks earlier, but I was still so comfortable with him, kissing him. Still mortally attracted to him, he had rebuffed me. I couldn't understand it. He had been hurt by my attempt to save what we had.

Men.

Craig was attempting to perform cunnilingus on me, but I was stiff and nervous and his stubble was hurting my most holy of holies. That's when Hazel intervened – and I was exceptionally grateful.

She made me cum. It didn't take very long but orgasming when one wants to and is not forced to, cumming at the hands – or, in this case, lips and tongue – of someone whom you permit to have that level of access to your vulnerable body was rapturous and my body shivered and shuddered as I threw my head back, gasping in delight and surprise. Was this what real sex was like?

What followed were pairing ups of couples, all having sex, then swapping eager partners and fucking some more. I didn't have sex with anyone. I sought out the comfort of Lucas and we kissed and fondled and giggled. I really liked him. I may have even loved him, but I didn't know enough about that particular subject to have formed a firm opinion.

After the gasping and groaning, the cocaine appeared, cut into six lines on a CD cover and resting precariously on the edge of the bed. Everyone had a turn schnarfing while my 'fuck it' switch tripped and I decided to partake even though I had never tried a hard illicit substance in my life. But I'd also never been licked out by a woman. It was just that kind of evening.

It was Lucas's turn, then mine. Then he sneezed. Hard. Both of our lines evaporated into the ether. We all laughed, though I was deeply disappointed, because I knew that doing cocaine for the first time too would have deepened the experience ten-fold.

Then, with an unusual absence of awkwardness, we all pulled our clothes back and returned to the lounge where the other guests had either left or stayed behind to rubberneck. We drank more cheap wine and danced to Edith a little more – this could not get any better, I thought.

I'm not sure how it happened. Whether Shaun and Craig persuaded Lucas to take the step or whether I was so inebriated that I just thought anything anyone said was a damn fine idea. But I ended up having sex with Lucas, just the two of us, in his room. It was somewhat painful and entirely pleasurable. Alone, without an audience, we fucked and laughed and he was tender and I was coquettish and it was an altogether loving experience.

When we returned to the lounge after a whole 10 minutes, it was to a rousing round of approving applause.

I did so love applause.

Up until that moment, it was the best night of my life.

I had lost my virginity to a girl and a boy on the same night.

And I had a massive hangover to show for it.

CHAPTER 17

Drinking, Drugs and Divorce

I was drinking full-time by the time my parents eventually got divorced. After 20 years of white-knuckling it together, they chose to part ways in the middle of my preliminary matric exams. Despite all those violent, loveless years, they chose a time when I needed to focus on the most important examinations of my school career.

My mother was the one who filed for divorce. The Sheriff of the Court had delivered the papers to my dad earlier that year after supper one evening. Enraged and confused, he took to his bedroom. By morning, everyone pretended it hadn't happened.

A few months later, they were set to appear in the magistrate's court to obtain a divorce based on "irreconcilable differences", which was code for "he cheats, he gambles, he lies, I hate him". They dropped me off at the entrance to the school and my first psychotic breakdown quietly took over. I walked straight through the campus and out the back gate and do not remember a thing until my father collected me at theatre school at 4 pm. It must have been a Tuesday because that was when drama class took place. I was emotional, weepy, randomly talking out loud to myself, soothing myself by stroking my upper arms. I was distraught.

This thing, this separation of the two of them, which I had wanted so badly for so long, had finally been concluded, and I was an absolute mess.

I vaguely remember smoking weed that day with my boyfriend, Christian, and his friend, Ryan (who later went on to kill himself by shooting himself in the head in front of his parents), but it's a murky recollection. I didn't like marijuana; I didn't like the surrender of control and increase in appetite. It messed with my body dysmorphia.

The weed wasn't the first illicit substance I had taken that year. That prize went to a black microdot that I had taken with Hazel and Marion at the National Arts Festival in Grahamstown. It was a few days after I had lost my precious virginity and the three of us decided to hitchhike to Grahamstown, nearly 900 kilometres from where we lived. I told my parents that I was getting a lift there and had suitable accommodation and they believed me – as they did most of my convincing lies. Maybe they just had to believe me because by this stage I was beyond their parental control.

One Saturday morning, for instance, I had wanted to go out, to hitchhike from the M5 freeway to town, in my two-tone, layered, ripped stockings and short black shorts and long-sleeved (always long-sleeved) jade-green top and my Docs (always my Doc Martens) and my mother had said "no", barricading the front door and threatening to accost me with a Teflon coated, heavy-based frying pan.

"Fuck you!"

It was the first time I had sworn directly at her. It felt unbelievably liberating. She stood frozen to the spot, shocked. Slowly, she lowered the frying pan to her side.

I pushed roughly past her and made my way to the highway so that I could hang out with my friends and then go dance like a lunatic and sip soda water at my new hangout The Stage, an alternative/Goth club on Loop Street in the city centre that played The Clash and Einstürzende Neubauten in equal amounts and on request. It opened at 5 pm, after theatre class.

They didn't have a proverbial leg to stand on, my parents. Their lives were unmanageable and so was their daughter.

So Marion, Hazel and I set off on our adventure – a cataclysmic disaster from the very start. In case we got attacked, we had a strategy to kill or maim the drivers. The plan was that Marion would sit in the passenger seat, me behind her in the back seat and Hazel behind the driver, holding a long-blade knife with which to slit the throat of any would-be attacker or rapist. If anyone could slice a jugular, it would be Hazel, despite being petite and blonde and resembling an actual pixie.

But we mistimed the trains, standing on the wrong end of the platform as the last train from Strand to closer-to-Grahamstown pulled in at the far end of the station – the side we were *not* waiting on. We raced down the platform and, as the train departed, Hazel and I managed to leap up onto the carriage, the doors held open by surprised passengers. We both turned around to see Marion still jogging alongside, about to run out of platform as the train picked up speed. She was not going to make it. Hazel and I, wordlessly, launched ourselves through the open doors of the carriage and landed awkwardly, heavily and – for Hazel – painfully on the tarred platform. We surveyed the damage; Hazel had scraped her thigh and her hand was bleeding, filled with tiny bits of gravel.

As the sun began to set, Hazel cried, Marion apologised and we all regrouped. Before it got dark, we would have to find the closest highway and hitchhike. We made our way from Strand Station and found the main freeway, stuck out our thumbs and waited; three young girls waiting for salvation.

That salvation came in the form of a bakkie, commandeered by a sympathetic farmer. The three of us had already created pseudonyms and a story to attach to our fantasy lives. We were at varsity – which he clearly didn't believe. He was a stud and wine farmer and he drove us to his farm. All fear of rape and assault flew out that bakkie window. We were just grateful to be off the darkening road and to have somewhere to sleep that night. His wife cleaned Hazel's wounds, fed us and sent us to bed. My bed had a patchwork eiderdown and the pillow was filled with feathers, which made me sneeze continuously on account of my allergy to all things avian. My explosive sneezes were accompanied by the eerie sounds of hooting owls in the trees outside.

The next morning, they fed us a huge breakfast. The farmer remarked on how his daughter was just a little older than us and that we should consider returning to Cape Town. Hazel said we would be pushing on, thank you. He dropped as at the turn-off to Caledon and it took us two more uneventful rides to reach the Grahamstown Botanical Gardens where we would spend the next few days tent-hopping (we obviously hadn't thought that far) and I would end up sleeping with Lucas the Ex, again.

I would take my first drug: LSD. I don't remember much. I do remember eating the most delicious, fine apricot jam out of a can and trying to find the bottom. I also remember the burning bush. We all saw it, the bush that was aflame but not burning. As we passed, it took on a sketchy animated appearance as though we were watching a graphic novel come to life. That we had all seen it baffled us beyond belief as we unpacked the trip in the early hours of the following morning. Surely we couldn't all have had the same hallucination? Wasn't that a primary rule of collectively tripping your tits off? Confused, but feeling a deep sense of connection, we continued talking shit until the sun rose on the misty public gardens.

I loved this drug. It was even better than the alcohol I had been consuming at a disturbing rate that year because of the alternative reality it produced. My father had instilled a rule that he preferred if I (and my brother and his friends) drank at home so that he had some semblance of control. So I drank frequently, sitting behind the purpose-built bar at one end of the garage, leaning against the maroon-padded vinyl construct, downing shots procured from the row of optics that were attached to a custom-built rotating stand. I drank anything except Red Heart Rum. Not rum. Never rum.

LSD, however, accessed parts of my mind that felt closed off and dusty, buried deep under intellectual overkill. It made me feel in turns paranoid and liberated. Acid was definitely a narcotic I could get behind. After the festival in Grahamstown, where we did not see a single theatrical production, we were fortunate enough to get a ride in a Safmarine cargo truck all the way to Cape Town. As I lay in the back of the cabin, jolted around by the speed at which the truck was careening down the highway, I knew I had found a drug that surpassed the pleasures of alcohol.

When I eventually got home, I realised I had left my small sling bag in the truck. A few days later, this mammoth 10-wheeler pulled up outside my house. My ID book had been inside the bag and the trucking team had tracked me down. I ran outside and retrieved it, thanking the driver and his co-pilot and waving them off.

"What was that all about?" enquired my father.

"Nothing."

"Why is a cargo truck dropping your bag off?" he persisted.

I acquiesced. "We hitchhiked to and from Grahamstown."

He smiled, forgetting himself, then replaced the expression with the appropriate scowl. "That is not okay. Go to your room."

There was a hint of pride in his voice that just could not be hidden.

After matriculating – and, to everyone's surprise, obtaining exceptional results – I applied to the University of Cape Town to do my Performer's Diploma. I even auditioned. But when the cheque for the acceptance fee was Returned to Sender because the date was incorrect, I declined my place. I didn't want to fail. I didn't want to be locked into another four years of studying. Also, I suspected my parents – post-divorce – couldn't afford the fees. So I rejected the institution's offer and no one tried to convince me otherwise. I decided to go work in a franchise steakhouse in Bergvliet and was much happier making my own money, or so I made myself believe. The cash allowed me freedom to drink more after shifts – as seems to be the tradition in the hospitality industry – and gave me the options of doing pretty much whatever the fuck I wanted: like go back to the National Arts Festival in Grahamstown the following July.

I met William on the bridge near the Village Green. I had returned to Grahamstown, but this time with new friends, and we stayed in an actual house, Casey's sister's shared digs. We even saw a play or two and a movie, *A Clockwork Orange*, which moved and frightened me to the bone. William was from the UK, so his accent titillated my very cells. He had kind, piercing blue eyes and unkempt blond hair stuffed under a blue-and-green peaked corduroy cap. He was travelling around Africa on his gap year in an old converted, lime-green Volkswagen kombi and had found his way to the festival. We locked eyes and I knew that I would be with him and put him through 47 types of hell.

We courted each other shyly, withholding the overwhelming role we both knew kismet had played. When the festival ended, I told my friends I'd be going up north to the Wild Coast with William. I phoned my father and said I'd be home in a few days. There was not much he could do or say. I asserted myself by settling in the front seat of the kombi, practically uninvited, along with a young Israeli girl and a Frenchman who were also travelling.

That Transkei trip was the best of my young life. I found my happy place in Coffee Bay and we spent a few idyllic days in a ramshackle house near the beach. We bought crayfish from over-enthusiastic vendors right by the ocean as we sunned ourselves in the scorching heat, knowing it was raining in every other part of the country. We wallowed in a bohemian eternity. William and I bonded and fucked and made plans for the future. I would come to the UK; he was enrolled at the University of Manchester and I would visit. I immediately agreed. I had to be with him, no matter where he was. When we left the Transkei and headed for Durban, where our fellow travellers took their leave, I was overcome with a deep depression. Over the next few days I refused to go home. I was obsessed and didn't want this fantastical journey to end. Eventually, William paid for a Translux bus ticket, forced me to onto it, and I reluctantly headed back to Cape Town. I spent the ride crying and listening to Counting Crows and Alanis Morissette on my headphones really loud, refusing to keep my stereo (or my grief) personal.

My dad was at the Cape Town bus terminus to collect me.

"You smell like a *kaffir*," he welcomed me.

I didn't care. I was going to find a way to get to William.

CHAPTER 18

Boomerang

I had always used the sheer intensity of my emotional range to manipulate and control. Going overseas was no exception. As part of the criteria for travelling to the UK, you had to have at least £500 in your bank account to pass through Customs at the airport. I did not have that amount of money. A lady I had heard about through Lucas often sent money abroad by depositing funds – plus a little extra for their trouble – into the accounts of young travellers, who would then deposit the funds in her UK bank account. Win-win.

By the time I was ready to depart, she no longer required my services. I was hysterical. Literally. My father had left on a business trip to Namibia the day before so my unwilling audience consisted of my mother and brother.

"You always want to ruin everything! You just want to control me! I said I would pay you back!" I shrieked. I had asked my mother for the money and she had said no.

I fled to my room and slid under my desk, clutching my knees and rocking aggressively and sobbing uncontrollably. I was heading for zealous overkill.

"No one loves me, no one loves me," I moaned.

My brother kneeled down and peered at me under the desk.

"You need to calm down," he whispered, unemotionally. I had heard him utter these words so many times over the years. He was the antithesis of me; he did not like brash displays of emotion; he did not like the idea that his sister's brain might snap at any given moment.

I continued rocking on my own pointless momentum, sobbing and wailing. I knew what I wanted and I was going to get it. My mother's expressionless face appeared under the melamine desk.

"Stop it," she ordered, less sensitively. "I'll give you the money tomorrow."

Game. Set. Match.

At the farewell dinner arranged by Auntie Sandy just before I departed for the UK in October 1995, I refused to eat the cheesecake she had gotten especially for me because it was my all-time favourite dessert. I was watching my weight. But later, when no one was looking, I scooped up a massive handful of cake, stuffed it in my mouth and ran straight to the bathroom where I wiped the filling from the sides of my mouth then followed through with my silent ritual of purging. Vomiting and not making a noise is a skill that cannot be taught.

I left for the UK a few days later with a packet of Thinz and a toothbrush in my overstuffed suitcase. Before seeing William I had made plans to stay with a friend, Emily, at her parents' house in Staines just outside of London. When I developed a horrendous cough, Emily took me to the pharmacy to get some cough mixture and in the aisle filled with nutritional shakes and multivitamins, my entire psyche cracked. You couldn't get slimming tablets in the UK without a prescription.

Apparently people were abusing diet tabs by putting speed in their beer and downing the chemical-laced liquid to get high at the pub. With the shocking realisation that I couldn't buy slimming tablets over the counter, I went on an all-out mission to get my hands on speed as often as possible. I wasn't working yet so I only had my savings. I didn't want to draw attention to myself but, where the fuck were all the dealers hiding?

As soon as I got to London, William began urging me to come up to Manchester, but I was being distracted: drinking and dropping acid in Camden. I was also constantly looking for a new place to stay because I couldn't live with Emily's parents indefinitely. So it was that Patrick, an old school friend from Abbotts, let me crash at his place in Bethnal Green, and it wasn't long before I ended up in his bed. Patrick and I were dangerously attracted to one another, but nothing had ever happened between us because "I had a boyfriend".

Eventually, of course, I ran out of money and Emily agreed to travel up to Manchester with me by coach to see William.

"Where the fuck have you been?" was my greeting – although it was accompanied by a long, languishing kiss that made Emily turn away, embarrassed.

We took up residence in his university digs, filled with boys from across the country who never cleaned the shower or the kitchen. Emily slept in an empty room – the original occupant had gone home for break – and I slept with William. That feeling of never wanting to leave him quickly returned and although I made three concerted attempts over a period of 10 days to board a coach back to London, each time I changed *our* minds at the eleventh hour. William and I were locked into one another on a neurological and cellular level. Our love was pure biochemistry. I was obsessed. It seemed mutual. It was bliss. Eventually, though, I did have to leave. Poverty and love are not supportive bedfellows.

And so I returned to London reluctantly, morosely, with angry, jilted Alanis still pumping full blast through my headphones, annoying my fellow passengers. I went to the au pair agency I had signed up with while still in South Africa and secured an interview in West Sussex. I landed the job at The All-England Jumping Course, looking after five children. I was 19 and could barely look after myself, and here I was watching kids.

Their father's wealth was a little overwhelming, but I truly adored the children. I would even smoke cigarettes behind the Conservatory or in my own private cottage with the eldest daughter who was 16 years old. She had two other blood siblings and their mother had hanged herself in the same Conservatory just over a year before. These kids were lovable, spoiled goods. I was nanny number 60-something.

It was Christmas Day, a few months into the job, and I was mopping the vast checkered kitchen floor, crying quietly to myself, homesick for Manchester, when I decided to leave. I had put on a massive amount of weight due to depression, lack of sunlight, eating packets of Hobnobs and an even greater scarcity of drugs of any description.

"I remember," the tyrannical father announced drunkenly at the expansive Christmas lunch table, "this skinny little girl arriving a few months ago and now look at her!" That was the nail in the au-pairing coffin. I took a train and coach up to Manchester to see William.

"We're driving down to my parents," he announced, obviously happy to see me. I panicked. I didn't do well with parents. Or, rather, I did initially, but then I quickly turned into the "bad influence" or "the slut that was fucking their son". I had no idea what to expect.

"They're lovely," he reassured me on the trip down in William's Land Rover Defender. "My dad's a farmer and they're both so down to earth."

I was not convinced. Anxiety tugged at every muscle. William drove expertly for the entire four and a half hours of heavy snow, but eventually we turned into a road – one that I soon realised was actually a long driveway that turned into a circular driveway, at the end of which rose a massive triple-storey manor house.

"Where are we?" I demanded, even though I already knew. I wanted to vomit.

"That's my house, Blacklands Hall," he replied, patting my trembling knee.

I felt instantly betrayed. He had money. His parents were rich. He hadn't told me. If there was one thing I was more intimidated by than parents it was parents with money.

William was right, though; they were both lovely and accepting and down to earth. His dad had a cheeky sense of humour and his mom was as sweet, cliché and kitsch as sequins. But I couldn't get over myself and my throbbing inferiority complex. I was awkward and uncomfortable and stuck to William like Velcro until we left.

* * *

"Do you want to get married?"

I scanned William's face. He was being as serious as a fatal illness. We had just returned from an unreal trip around Europe in his converted Land Rover: Italy, Greece, Germany, Switzerland, France, Turkey, the Netherlands. I had fallen madly in love with Rome and Istanbul, despite having been sexually assaulted in Turkey. My working holiday visa was way past its expiry and none of my friends wanted me to leave. Getting married to stay in the UK sounded like an excellent idea. I had already been home and back again. My second sojourn had not been remotely as exciting as the first. I had secured a normal boring job, waitressing at Yo Yo's, an Asian restaurant-bar-club in Manchester, and initially shared William's room in a proper house he and his uni mates had rented in the suburbs. I felt trapped and suffocated. I threw in dramatic events like attempted suicides and overdoses to try to spice things up. I became immovable and intolerable but still William hung onto his love for me despite my histrionics.

Finally William and I decided it best that we not live together any more. Familiarity had definitely bred a fungal kind of contempt. I decided to move to Salford with my friend Ella and bagged myself an equally mind-numbing waitressing job in the city. Ella and I played grown-up. I celebrated my twenty-first birthday on 19 October 1997 with seven bottles of Moët & Chandon, which I didn't really share. Princess Diana died horrifically and senselessly, and the mourning nation reflected my internal mood.

I swallowed the vomit that had collected in my mouth when William popped the question. "Sure, let's look into it."

It wasn't hard to find a marriage office in the middle of the city. They even gave us a shiny brochure and we set a date for three days from then. For the next 24 hours, we debated the pros and cons. Alicia Phillips was the voice of reason.

"Don't be ridiculous," she said. "You're too young to get married and it's for the wrong reason."

Alicia was the closest thing I had to a best friend; she had also reconfirmed my bisexuality one drunken night out with her boyfriend. But that experience did not affect our friendship in any way, though I couldn't understand why William had been so upset when I told him, rather casually, about our delicious encounter.

The night before the proposed wedding day, William's pallor started turning a strange hue of green. By that stage, every boy in the house had offered to marry me to help me stay in the UK, which was both flattering and endearing.

"Let's not do this," I offered, testing the premarital waters.

He let out a huge sigh of what was obviously relief. "You sure?" he asked.

I wasn't.

"Of course. It's a stupid idea. I'll just go home and we'll make a plan." He smiled for the first time in three days. I was quietly devastated.

I returned home much heavier and poorer.

"You've gotten so fat," my mother hugged me with barely bent elbows and angled her face so I could kiss her on her icy cheek.

"Things have changed here," my mother continued, warning me in the car on the drive home. She rambled on about PAGAD and increased violence and crime as I looked out the window at the sepia-tinted, William-less world.

My cousin Tyra had been at the airport and promised to phone me. She wasn't really my cousin. Her mother, Sandy, was my mother's cousin. But in the name of simplification, Tyra was my cousin, just a couple of years younger than me. She did as she had promised and I tried to acclimatise to what should have been a familiar space.

"Do you want to come with me to a party tomorrow night?" she asked.

I held the phone receiver between my ear and shoulder, twirling the tangled cord just as I had done a few years prior. Nothing had changed. Everything was still fucking beige.

"I don't think so …"

"Please?" she begged. "It's Carl Cox at The Three Arts. It's going to be amazing."

The Three Arts? That dilapidated old theatre. Why would I want to go there? To listen to a progressive house DJ from the country I just came from?

But I was deeply depressed so I agreed. Tyra yelped with excitement.

"We'll pick you up at 10 tomorrow night." That was bedtime for me, but I was bored and intrigued and happy for the chance to get out the beige house.

When Tyra and her boyfriend picked me up at 10.30 pm, she jumped out the passenger seat as they pulled up and ran inside to greet my mother and brother then half-dragged me to the car.

"Oh my God! Oh my God!" she squealed in her New York accent tinged with the best parts of a South African one. "I can't wait!"

Italian-American by birth with an undeniable coloured heritage, Tyra was skinny and beautiful and affable and lovable, charming accent and all. I decided that spending a few hours with her wouldn't be so bad. When we arrived at The Three Arts, the parking lot was packed to capacity and her boyfriend ramped up a little hill behind the venue and parked on the slope.

Tyra turned around to face me.

"You want an eccie?"

I was genuinely surprised. She took drugs? I had taken my first Ecstasy pill at the very famous nightclub, The Hacienda, in Manchester and two more pills subsequently. I had loved the loved-up experience. I had loved the anticipation of 'coming on' and the subsequent rush of heady happiness and the instant soul connection between me and the music, as well as the loss of all sensual inhibitions. I loved loving everything and everyone and grinding my jaw and grinning like a fool until it felt as though my teeth would crack. And dancing. I loved the manic, marathon dance sessions, bopping and grooving and sharing bottles of water and knowing smiles with complete strangers. I had by this stage admitted my love and devotion for all things narcotic but my inability to secure a steady line of drugs back in the UK had made me feel trapped like the sky between rooftops.

"Sure…?" I answered, uncertainly.

She handed me a white pill with three diamonds in a triad stamped on one side while popping her own in her mouth and chasing it with water. She inserted one in her boyfriend's mouth and he took the bottle from her and swallowed the pill. I accepted the bottle and downed mine too.

"Don't forget to drink lots of water," she said as we exited the car and joined the snaking line of revellers slowly making their way to the entrance. The floor of the foyer was covered with strips of luminous material and pillows. A few people lay or sat in the makeshift space and Tyra waved to a few.

"Let's sit here until we come on," she suggested.

She held my hand as we navigated the pillows and people, found a corner and nestled into the material strips, which felt like bits of wetsuit. She kept passing me the water bottle and motioning me to drink, which I obediently did. She handed me a piece of chewing gum as though she was dispensing vital, chronic medicine.

"You'll need this. Chew. I have more for later."

From our vantage point in what she called "The Chill-Out Room" I started recognising people: my blood cousins, Trevor and André, Lila – a year ahead of me at school – and another girl who had been in my class at Springfield, as well as Lloyd, on whom I had had a crush since I was 15, kids from my neighbourhood; everyone was there and greeted me enthusiastically.

What the fuck was going on?

Soon I started feeling the effects of the E: the tingling up and down my spine, the 'growing pains' in my limbs that were anything but painful, the tightening in my jaw, my stomach feeling as though it wanted to eject its contents and the dryness of my mouth. And the music! Music that I couldn't previously hear from the stage upstairs suddenly flooded my ears and I felt overwhelmingly obligated to get up and find the source. Tyra looked at me, straight in the eyes, her eyelids fluttering, grinning stupidly and vibrating with excitement.

"It's on!"

CHAPTER 19

The Sunrise Set

My mother had been right: things had very definitely changed while I'd been away. That night at Carl Cox was unreal, not only in the potency of the Ecstasy, which surpassed anything I'd had before, but in the realisation that everyone I knew in Cape Town was happily fucked on pills and other narcotics on what seemed a permanent basis. It was beautiful: seeing the familiar smiles, grinding jaws and rolling eyes, hugging the known and unknown. Nearly blinded and suffocated by strobe lights and lasers and artificial smoke, the offer of water and shoulder rubs from complete strangers, the unmistakable smell of Tiger Balm pervading the air and burning my skin on contact. Superb singeing that just pushed the drug even further. And dancing. Every song hooked into my heart as though it had been produced Just For Me. It would have been rude not to dance.

So we danced.

The disaffected, fearless, fucked-up youth danced.

That night at The Three Arts we danced until the sun rose. And so it was every weekend. Paul Oakenfold at Sasani Studios, which we entered via a realistic-looking sky bridge, Tsuyoshi Suzuki at Longkloof Studios, where the walls pulsated and seemed to sweat along with us, Carl Cox's triumphant return to The Three Arts, and Sasha and John Digweed at the same overloaded venue. It was meant to hold 2500 people but at least 6000 were in jubilant attendance. And then there was The Three Gables ...

We lost our minds on a frequent and purposeful basis. I made deep and drug-induced friends with old friends, I made friends with family, I made friends with new friends.

I was home. More home than I had ever been. Drugs were the great equaliser and I finally felt like I truly belonged. I belonged in the dewy fynbos of Newlands Forest, lying down in the grass and coming down from the pills at sunrise; I belonged on the back seat of friends' cars sliding more Ecstasy down my throat at 3 am; I belonged in the houses of strangers, snorting their cocaine at 1 pm and rambling on about the point of toes at the end of one's feet; I belonged outside Synergy on New Year's morning kissing a beautiful blond boy, a total stranger, on a whim; I belonged in Jules Jenneke's car listening to music no one had ever heard of but everyone would soon; I belonged in the corners of laser-lit, smoke-filled clubs kissing girls and boys alike, driven by the loved-up lust of Ecstasy; I belonged alongside Diana Millar, "Queen of Clubs", her trusty sidekick and inseparable confidante doing more cocaine in the 'offices' of heaving clubs; I belonged just five metres from Carl Cox on the stage when he made his return to Cape Town, squeezing Trevor's hand with exhilaration and trying not to vomit again from the pills; I belonged on top of quivering speakers where I danced and danced, doing even more of other people's drugs in toilet stalls, wiping the top of the cisterns as though that would magically make them hygienic; I belonged in the divine and delirious haven of Dulverton Road – before and after a riotous night – doing more drugs until it was Sunday and we would all watch *Dawson's Creek* at 4 pm knowing that it would soon be time to go home; I belonged kapping buttons – smoking a combination of Mandrax and weed – with the Lansdowne boys in the station subway, ert-ing – drooling on myself in a state of intoxicated semi-consciousness – and vomiting and burning my fingers on the bottleneck pipes; I belonged naked, hiding in the kitchen of the basement flat of a boy whose his girlfriend was on the hunt; I belonged in the back of a police van, arrested for public indecency after starting a drunken threesome in the back of a friend's car outside Westerford Spar in the middle of the night; I belonged at the Mary Stopes clinic, alone, having my first secret abortion; I belonged in the bedrooms of boys who had girlfriends, making out passionately and guilt-free with them to prove a salient point about relationships of which only I'm aware; I belonged in my bed – having been awake for two days – crying myself to unattainable sleep. I belonged by myself in my room doing drugs on my own.

In whatever form it took, I belonged.

In my desperate search for belonging, I fucked everything with two legs and a heartbeat. Heartbeat optional. My lust looked like desperation, like the unrequited need to be loved it so transparently was. Every drunken moan and faked groan and exaggerated sigh deepened my need to please him or her, my need to connect and translate sex into love. And after, there would be that pervasive, unmistakable smell of sex, of mistakes, of urgency, of what should not have been; and I would taste his potent cum in my mouth or her sweet sex and I would need a drink to forget. I would feel the tinge of shame and the burn of regret, knowing – without a shadow of a doubt – that I would be doing it all over again. Soon.

We shouldn't be doing this.

I know.

I'm married. I told you that.

I know.

We really shouldn't be doing this.

But, baby, we already are.

I invited and fed off complexity. I longed for stability but, like a dirty thought in a clean mind, I felt hopelessly out of place in the realm of normality.

One friend tried to warn me: "You know that the only thing attractive about married men is their unavailability?"

I shook my head and slowly exhaled a plume of grey-white smoke, then chewed on my bottom lip. "But I need to test the weaknesses of their relationship. I'm doing them a public service."

"You'll get hurt."

"Probably. Yes … always."

I developed a magnetic radar for every move of the very married man, and he for mine. Tracking each other from across a room, orbiting around another, thriving on stolen glances and clandestine touches. Craving closeness but so achingly distant. It could never be anything other than what it was: a whispered secret, a furtive tryst. It was a fractured sort of love. It was a perfect disaster. I knew that, but not doing it would be unthinkable.

I need to see you.

You can't. She'll be there.

I stood bolt upright when I read his response to my text. I knocked over the mug of strong, black coffee and it dripped down the side of the counter, forming a sticky, shallow pool on the white tiled floor. So very careless, so very messy.

I don't care. I'm coming anyway.

And I did. I went to that damned cliquey cocktail party. I immediately recognised The Wife. Putting a face to an unspoken name had never been that painful. The Wife threw her head back when she laughed, her hair swishing elegantly like those girls in the shampoo commercials. She was territorially close to him, touching his arm lightly at the elbow. He avoided my searching gaze and shifted uncomfortably from one foot to the other, sipping repeatedly from an empty glass long finished.

I needed to leave this place.

A wasted friend grabbed the cuff of my coat and pulled me towards the two.

"Have you met Natalie?"

"Yes, I think we've met before ..."

"Pleased to meet you, but I don't think we have ... Have we?"

Except for her lopsided smile, The Wife's face was flawless, sickeningly beautiful and horrendously endearing. Her skin was soft and her fingers long and slender; fingers that had touched him too. I didn't want to let go of that hand; I wanted The Wife to feel my craving and my pain, to transfer what I had felt by emotional osmosis.

I had to leave this place.

The room hung heavy with misguided memories. I needed to

leave, was desperate to leave – the kind of desperation people feel when they need to leave a house after a death or a divorce. I clambered into my car, gripped the steering wheel tightly with both hands and banged my forehead on it twice, hard. I let out a tortured whimper, turned the key in the ignition and drove, directionless. I needed to find a place where I would feel comfortable enough to have a nervous breakdown.

CHAPTER 20

Swings and Roundabouts

Driving away from that party, I was a psychotic, terrifying mess. But that was nothing new.

My childhood had seen me throwing tantrums of monumental proportions if I did not get my own way, if I felt slighted or that the world was treating me unfairly. Like on my brother's birthdays when, when he received his present from my parents, I would go postal because of the injustice of it all. I could not fathom why I should not also receive a gift and eventually, to avoid histrionics, my parents acquiesced and started buying me gifts on his birthday too. Justice was restored, hysterical child placated. Except on his thirteenth birthday when he received a real bicycle (with gear changes – which no one actually ever knew how to use). I was incensed.

"Why couldn't you get that for him for Christmas?" I screeched, running into the garage and kicking my old BMX. "Why couldn't you wait for Christmas so we could both get a new bike?"

I cried all the way to my room, stripped down to my unsightly nakedness, donned my swimming costume and headed for the pool. I swam endless laps for hours, crying and holding my breath then let out deep bubbly high-pitched bawls under the surface until I was exhausted and emotionally spent.

Water, I had found, was soothing and no one can hear you scream when you're under.

Throughout my childhood I would lie in the bathtub and slowly start filling the bath with hot, then even boiling water until my skin burned, turning brown-red. The pain was excruciating, every part of me felt like it had been doused in petrol and set alight, but somehow it alleviated all the agony I felt inside.

My adolescent years were filled with equally excessive emotional outbursts, unfounded mood swings and spectacular melodramas. I would jump from manic to depressive like Tarzan swinging on jungle vines. I had no control over myself, and everyone else had even less control over me – because of her disdain for crying or any display of emotion, my mother especially despised my emotional outbursts. I had no understanding of my erratic, manic behaviour and no one tried to help me come to grips with it.

"She's just being herself."

"She's just having one of her fits."

"Maybe she's hyperactive?"

"She's just being moody."

She was just being bipolar. I only discovered that word later.

To their credit, after the divorce when I was 17 and due to my mini-psychotic response, my parents sent me to my second psychologist. It was the school's alternative to insisting on a drug test. I knew I would fail, but our GP claimed it was illegal to request a drug test unless I was being an actual disruption to the school. I actually broke out in sweat from relief in the doctor's rooms. The headmaster at Abbotts, after reminding me that he was only allowing me this reprieve because of my brother's brilliant legacy, told my father that I needed (lowered, stern voice) "psychological help". I had to go or face expulsion. I went for two sessions, successfully managing to say absolutely nothing, not a word, my peak cap pulled way over my eyes to block the psychologist's attempts at fixing me. He terminated the therapy, that young, hapless, out-of-his-depth psychologist and referred me on to a psychiatrist who prescribed Eglonyl, an antidepressant, my very first – but by no means last – psychiatric medication. It did nothing for me except make me lactate, the unwanted milk running freely from my nipples, leaving embarrassing wet stains on my tops. I wore black from then on, though most people thought I was being purposefully Gothic or depressive.

As I got together with boys (and girls) my behaviour in all relationships was erratic and trying. I constantly tested boundaries and pushed the envelope of 'normal girlfriend' conduct. I couldn't comprehend my own behaviour within the confines of a romantic partnership, but I knew that real and fake attempted suicides, real and fake miscarriages and staging domination/submission (read: rape) scenarios were not normal. I would often pretend to be asleep or in a state of sleepwalking while allowing someone to fuck me. I woke up some mornings from shambolic one-night stands. I indulged in histrionics brought on by the slightest of slights, screaming matches where I was the only one doing any screaming, throwing car keys over balconies into bushes and once attempting to swallow a front-door key to block an escape in the throes of a fight. I found myself walking to the petrol station on my own in one of the most dangerous neighbourhoods in Manchester to buy cigarettes at 3 am because William refused to after I woke him – having been staring at him and plotting his demise for a few hours. All of this was tolerated because I attracted men – and later women – with just the right pathology to fit perfectly into my manic-depressive puzzle piece.

Then I met Helen. My reign of emotional terror continued unabated until she left for Australia when I was 22.

That's how I landed up in a clinic for the first time.

"Why are you here?"

"I can't stop crying."

"Why? What happened?"

"She left, my girl— best friend left, and I can't stop crying."

"Do you use drugs?"

I furrowed my brow and gave the best incensed look I could muster. I wasn't going to fall into that trap again. That question had secured my bed at the clinic. On the day that Helen took the train to Johannesburg and left me, the tears started and didn't stop. Work sent me home and after a few hours of ceaseless sobbing, my parents took me to our family GP, Dr Salie, to whom – thinking our conversation was confidential – I had disclosed my excessive drug use. He had gotten up from his chair behind the vast faux oak desk, walked to the door of his consulting room and opened it to call my mother to join us.

She had barely sat down next to me when he said, "Desiree has been using a lot of drugs. She needs to be admitted to a clinic."

I wanted to scream, horrified by the betrayal, but all I could manage was more sobbing. I had no more words.

"Do I use *drugs*?" I asked incredulously, as though I had misheard the question.

The psychiatrist nodded.

"No. Never." I shook my head vigorously. That's not why I was in the clinic.

"Tell me about her, your best friend."

I crossed my legs in the smoothly upholstered seat of the big wingback armchair – my now habitual position in psychologists' and psychiatrists' chairs. I thought it made me look smaller, younger, less likely to be responsible for my own chaos. I seriously pondered the question despite the fuzziness of my brain.

I wanted to say: we met while working as waitresses at Mugg & Bean at the Waterfront and we clicked instantly, a soul connection. I wanted to say that she had been travelling solo around the world and I felt lucky that she chose Cape Town when she did and that we had met. I wanted to say that I loved her and my heart was in pieces that she had left to carry on travelling, to Australia of all fucking places. I wanted to say that she was straightforward and funny and her smile made my heart light up. I wanted to say that she made me feel corny and foolish with love and lust. I wanted to say that I was in love with her even though she treated our relationships as 'friends with benefits', without a trace of malice. I wanted to say, I was the first girl she ever kissed, in the darkness of the outside courtyard at Angel's nightclub. I wanted to say that I couldn't imagine carrying on without her.

But, instead, I said, "I miss her. A lot."

Which was true, of course, but I had been crying now for three days, stopping only when they sedated me – which I looked forward to like scones and clotted cream at High Tea.

On admission, the nurse had said, "Get into your pyjamas before you take these," and handed me a little plastic cup containing two yellow hexagonal pills. "And get into bed. Otherwise you're going to hurt yourself."

I didn't believe her. I had been playing around recreationally with Valium and Ativan and Dormicum and, my favourite, Rohypnol. Nothing could be *that* potent. But she was right. I got undressed, neatly folding the musky, stained clothes I had refused to change out of for the last two days and placed them into the cupboard, snapping the padlock shut. Still sobbing, snot running into my mouth, I slipped into pale turquoise satin pyjamas that weren't mine. My mother had packed my bag, clearly. It seemed important to her that I dress appropriately during my nervous breakdown. I pulled back the covers of the bed made up to military perfection and slipped into the clean sheets, sliding my padlock key under my pillow. I held the little plastic container to my lips and threw back the contents. I washed it down with water from the glass that rested on a saucer. Very fancy. And that was the last thought I remembered.

When I woke up, nearly 10 hours later and facing the wrong way on the dishevelled bed, I made a mental note to find out the name of those pills. The next day, for some unknown reason, my temperature spiked dangerously and I felt horrendous. I wasn't about to tell anyone that I was actually detoxing and as the ambulance, sirens blaring, rushed me to the nearest Medi-Clinic I knew I wouldn't utter a word of truth in that place.

I was dished out lots of very super calming drugs by Dr Muller, my assigned psychiatrist, nicknamed the "Benzo Gnome" for his free and loose approach to prescribing Benzodiazapines. I shuffled around the clinic in my slippers. I was a slipper shuffler, like my dad. Heels pressed down on the backs of the slippers instead of inside the shoe. Shloof-shloof-shloof-shloof. He drove my mother crazy.

"Why the fuck can't the man just pick up his feet?" she would complain to me, but never to him.

I made a frame out of papier-mâché in Art Therapy. I told the occupational therapist, tears welling up in my blurry eyes, that I had such a chronic low self-esteem (sob, sob, get handed a box of tissues, soothing pat on the shoulder). I snuck cigarettes to the Eating Disorder patients and was jokingly berated by the Addictions patients that I was definitely in the wrong unit.

My first psychiatric admission was, by all accounts, fun and relaxing – except for the unplanned and unpermitted exorcism. During visiting hours, under the massive tree that grew in the front garden – and in full view of the other patients and their loved ones – my uncle Albert, a lay minister, and his friend laid hands on me and prayed.

"Satan, remove thyself from this child, your child, this child of Jesus."

This what? My eyes were shut tightly against this debacle. I refused to believe it was happening.

"Wash away all traces of evil, of addiction, Lord Jesus," he continued.

My mother was sitting on the bench next to me, which was tilted at a slight angle as if the roots of the gigantic tree had shown it who was boss. She clutched my hand, fervently willing sanity and decency into me by osmosis as she uttered "Amen" after every Godly direction that was issued.

"Holy Spirit," he bellowed, "enter this child and cleanse her soul."

Jesus wept. I wept. I began crying again, howling. Hot tears of public humiliation streamed down my cheeks. I imagined all the patients and visitors pressing their faces up against the glass of the sunroom, dumbfounded as the spectacle unfolded. The stranger's hand was also upon me and he was also amen-ing away. All I wanted was for it to be over and, finally, it ended.

"Don't worry," Uncle Albert reassured everyone, "crying is normal. It's the Devil being released."

I opened my eyes and looked up at my father, and remember feeling utterly betrayed. The previous evening, as I sat next to him on the one-seater chair, we stretched our arms out and realised for the first time that we had identically shaped fingers. I felt, as I hadn't in a long time, that I was his girl again. But now he was a traitor. A crooked-fingered traitor.

I got up from the bench and half-ran upstairs to the nurses' station and asked for "something for anxiety please", which I obtained from the concerned nurse-on-duty and went to my room and cried more into my pillow.

Fuck Jesus.

And fuck my uncle. This was unforgivable. Mentally, I buried that resentment deep in my emotional filing system to be used at a later stage.

I was discharged after two weeks … and readmitted three days later. I couldn't adapt to the outside, which was alarming because I thought the clinic had had no real effect on me. But on discharge I had felt even more depressed, more anxious, more psychotic. I wanted to murder my parents in their bed and kill myself – by overdose, of course.

And then, after two days back, I discharged myself again – still sans a true diagnosis. I wanted – needed – proper drugs again.

PART 3

Fuck the Rules

CHAPTER 21

The Meeting

Lucas, my short-term ex-boyfriend, and I became fuck buddies. I'd been back in SA for two years, and in that time things had gotten a whole lot worse, though I of course remained blissfully oblivious to this decline. We were now on our way to score pills and coke in Woodstock for the New Year's Eve celebrations, the heralding in of the Millennium. We were going to need a whole lot of drugs to get wasted.

It was a scorching summer's day and, as we drove down Kloof Street, the window wound all the way down to let the cool breeze blow through Lucas's fucked-up, old, air-conditioner-less car, I did my routine scan of the passing vehicles on the street, searching for another vehicle; a lime-green 1970s' VW kombi with a white roof. I knew I wouldn't see it, but a part of me always hoped. I had been waiting for William, to see that car, for months.

The breeze kissed my cheeks and whipped my hair around my face. The heat of the day mixed with alcohol made me smile. Faith Evans's 'Love Like This' was blasting through the crackly front speakers.

I never knew there was a love like this before ...

I stretched my hand out of the car window and flapped it up and down in the wind in time to the music.

Fuck, this all felt so good. This felt so very summer. I reached my other hand over and squeezed Lucas's knee.

"I'm really sorry about your hair," I offered again.

He ran his hand through the crater I had created with my kitchen scissors. "It's okay. You can hardly notice the hole."

"Maybe."

I kept my hand on his knee and squeezed again. He smiled. I liked it when he smiled with his big brown eyes. I really liked him. He was cute and funny and sensitive and smart and comfortable. I think I loved him. But not in a senseless, over-emotional kind of way.

The sex was fabulous. Non-threatening, non-traumatising, affectionate fucking. The friends-with-benefits arrangement worked so well. I didn't consider my carnal dalliances with either sex as cheating. I allowed myself off on a technicality. That technicality being that I was merely having occasional and convenient sexual relations with very good, non-threatening male and female friends whom he did not know. What *was* cheating was William fucking my very good friend, Alicia, on not one, but two occasions in some backwater in Sussex. That was in-fucking-fidelity right there. I also didn't disclose to William the numerous sexual and pseudo-sexual affairs I had had with a litany of other men and women while we were apart, but somehow I justified them all to myself. The double standards did not elude me but the denial comforted me.

I had given William an ultimatum: come to Cape Town to sort things out and reclaim our relationship, or it was over. He was a tour guide on trans-continental tours somewhere in Africa that always ended in Cape Town, and I had waited seven months for him to arrive, to see that kombi, for him to show his true intent. On some subconscious level, I had set a deadline of New Year's Eve of the year 2000. I don't remember doing it but, as Lucas and I drove up Roodebloem Road to meet the dealer, my heart felt simultaneously constrictively tight and enlarged. I decided to let William go. Four years of an intercontinental and long-distance relationship later and it was over. For me, anyway.

I was ready to move on.

1 January 2000. 7 am.

I had never seen such yellow cocaine before and my eyes had most certainly never come to rest on anything quite like *him* before. I was disproportionately excited at the sight of both. His six-foot frame reclined across the bed in the spare room of the apartment, like some latter-day Botticelli poster boy. He was chopping lines of clumpy golden cocaine.

He seemed to be holding court – him and his sunshine-yellow cocaine; three or four wide-eyed partygoers were perched on the edge of the bed, one cross-legged on the floor, all chatting incessantly and waiting eagerly while he expertly chopped lines on the CD cover using an ATM card.

He had the most beautiful hands I had ever seen: slender, soft, milky white fingers that looked as though they could conjure pure magic out of nothing at all. His cheeks were tinged slightly pink and his eyes, like the rest of ours, were red-rimmed from the night of abundant excess, but still beguiling. He had a mop of fine, straight dark brown hair, a lock of which periodically fell across his eye and he kept pushing it away even when it wasn't there.

I stood in the doorway, feeling like the voyeur that I was, an unwelcome intruder on this private party. I was about to turn to leave when he looked up and smiled, his big hazel eyes narrowing slightly at the corners.

"Hey. Come in. You want a line?"

I want you.

"Yes, please, sure," I responded instead.

He patted an open space on the bed next to him and I climbed over an inappropriately dressed girl seated on the floor and sat cross-legged in the space he'd made for me. I felt a powerful magnetic pull towards him – on a deeply cellular level – and I wondered whether he felt it too. He handed me a tightly rolled-up bank note and held up the CD cover to just below my chin, which I quickly scanned, identifying the biggest line from the almost uniform ones on it. With my left hand, I bunched my curly hair into a loose ponytail behind my head, leaned forward and, holding the note with my right, snorted.

I released my hair, leaned back and smiled broadly, then sniffed.

"Fucking hell!"

"Good, yeah?" he asked, already knowing the answer.

"Oh, yeah."

"Want some more?"

I want you.

"I won't say no. I'm Desiree, by the way." I felt immediately self-conscious.

"I'm Darren. Everyone calls me DJ."

I smiled. I could feel the warmth permeate from his body, mere centimetres from mine. I never wanted to move again.

My friends and I had ended up in *Someone's* flat *Somewhere* in Cape Town. Green Point or Bantry Bay, maybe. I could definitely hear the lulling roll of ocean waves in the distance. The apartment was well appointed and dimly lit by the silver-grey daylight; and I had just seen the first sunrise, sort of, of the millennium a few hours before so it must have been early morning.

I wasn't sure who I had arrived with or how I had gotten there.

New Year's Eve celebrations had been a blissful blur, to say the least. I sat at the end of the overstuffed cream couch, sipping on a fluted glass of sparkling wine, trying to piece together the night's events but the memories remained wispy and elusive.

I know at one point I had insisted on going home and changing my clothes. That's how I found myself in red capri pants and a white mesh vest with ornate floral embroidery and black kitten heels. I had had sex with Lucas at midnight. We were trying to be all symbolic and "go in with a bang", but we had had far too much cocaine and he made me promise not to tell anyone that he hadn't cum. I had just laughed and cut another line. Who actually cared? And then there was the party at Café Bardeli and all that lovely champagne and more coke even though, Jesus, the line to the one bathroom there was ridiculously long. Then the beach for sunrise, where we realised we were on the completely wrong side of the peninsula to witness the dawn and then …

A complete blank.

I just did not know.

What I did know was that I had consumed an unreal amount of narcotics and alcohol the entire night and morning, and was showing no signs of abating. I was currently at the tail end of my fourth Ecstasy pill and starting to believe heavily in religion. Not the organised kind, of course. That would have been silly.

I desperately needed a change of scenery. The lounge was becoming claustrophobic, the music blaring from the makeshift decks not in tune with my particular buzz, and there was a definite smell of mandrax emanating from the balcony, which made me slightly nauseous, so I wandered down the hallway, intent on a daring exploration and feeling very heroic for going on my own.

When I found him in that spare bedroom, I could have sworn I heard a choir of off-key angels singing "Hallelujah!" If I hadn't been so gutter-drug-fucked, I may have realised it was actually the wail of police sirens.

CHAPTER 22

The Crossroads

"Get the fuck out of my car!" Darren yelled.

We had been 'seeing' each other for two weeks now. My millennium obsession. By that I mean I had basically been stalking him. I couldn't let go of the sticky notion that we were meant to be together. So I would magically appear wherever he was DJ-ing, which wasn't that abnormal if you followed Diana Millar's "Queen of Clubs" column in the evening newspaper's entertainment supplement. Despite being tactile-defensive and hating the feel of newspaper, I would scan the column and know exactly where he would be playing the entire week. More often than not though, I would find him at the sublime club, Rhythm Divine, where he played regularly. I would sit on a barstool at the window, overlooking Long Street, waiting to see his car pull up outside. I would feign surprise when I saw him and greet him, melting at his touch when he hugged me. I would make it look like a coincidence that we were running into each other so frequently. Once I infiltrated his personal space, I stuck to him like white on rice. I did what I did best: I morphed myself into the perfect version of what I thought he wanted me to be. I wanted him and I knew I was going to get what I wanted.

"I said, get the fuck out. Now!"

This, however, was not what I wanted.

"Dude," said Brad, turning to look at my stunned face from his position in the passenger seat, "that's a bit harsh."

I was too shocked to understand Brad was being nice to me. I was too shocked to remember, as I fumbled to unlock the back door, that the car had central locking. I was too shocked to have even realised that we were parked outside my apartment block. It was 6 am but the sun was being all proudly African, bright light and stifling heat already streaming into the car and giving the old BMW's air-con a run for its money. We had left the club about an hour before and had been driving around Vredehoek and Gardens, stopping on the side of the road, Brad chopping lines on a CD cover and pushing the boundaries of getting high while watching the sparkling waters lap against the sloping concrete sides of Molteno Reservoir or staring out of the windows at the small empty swings and plastic slides of Deer Park. Darren was in the driver's seat.

"I said, get the fuck out. Now!"

Tears had collected and pooled in my lower lids. Usually my tear ducts didn't function when I was this intoxicated, so that shocked me too. I wiped them away with the back of my clammy wrist.

"I can't open the door," I whispered, hoarsely.

Click, click.

I slung my small bag over my shoulder and exited, slamming the door as hard as I could. I walked up the three steps to my complex's security gate and, burning with confusion and humiliation, turned to look at him through the tinted windscreen and screamed, "Fuck you!" while searching the depths of my tiny bag for my keys. My retort had been lost on him – he was already revving the engine and careering off down the road, his back tyres spinning.

I located the keys under the not-much-at-all that the bag held and they dropped from my trembling hands to the dusty gravel at the gate.

"Fuuuuuuuuck!" I cried out to no one in particular. A luminous green-and-yellow Lycra-clad cyclist whizzed past, completely unaware of my morning mortification. Fucking cyclists.

I retrieved the keys from the ground and, in tears, marched to my flat on the first floor. I unlocked the door quietly and tiptoed in, unsure of whether my housemate was even home. Then, perched on the edge of my futon, I tried to make sense of the evening's events. It was hard; I was high as a motherfucker.

I had 'run into' Darren at the club. Okay, stalked him. Again. Check.

He had been DJ-ing and, for most of the night, ignoring me, save for the occasional abrupt exchange in the cramped toilet stall. Check.

I had had a long, deep conversation with an old male acquaintance on the threadbare couch near the club's door. I hadn't seen him in years. Check.

Darren had gotten *dik* upset that I had been speaking to another man. Check.

Once Willem, the club owner, had paid him for his set, he told me to get into the car. Check.

Then he kicked me the fuck out of his car. Check.

I lay back on the bed and sobbed. Check.

At some point I must have fallen into a fitful sleep, because when I woke up it was already dark, but I was still exhausted. I removed my sticky clothes and took a long, hot shower under the shower head from hell. Too hot, not enough pressure. I pulled on tracksuit pants and a hoodie, searched the fridge and found some of my flatmate's expensive wine, poured myself a generous glass, then found an A4 foolscap pad and a pen and got comfortable on the deep, cream sofa. Then I did what anyone in my situation would do: I wrote a five-page letter to the God. More a hostage negotiation than a pure-intentioned epistle. I wanted some things and I offered, sincerely and determinedly, to do some things in return, to change some things about my life: my eating habits, sleeping habits, my drug habits. I wrote four pages of promises, then laid down the paper and pen. I poured another glass of wine and downed it.

Dare I ask for it? Could I be so presumptuous as to bargain with God?

I stood up, retrieved the pen and paper and moved to the outside balcony, taking a huge gulp of wine as I walked. I settled into a chair and wrote:

I want a monogamous, healthy & happy (no, ecstatic!), fulfilling, loving relationship. I want The One. I want the big, Big Love. I want the give and receive. I want mutual bliss and lessons & more love. If I am not ready, I understand. Please give me the clarity of heart & mind to recognise it and the strength to let it go if it isn't. Allow me to see people & relationships for what they are & allow me to learn the lessons that each one brings. Help me to learn that I can be alone & be happy. Help me not to make decisions based on desperation & insecurity. I just want to be loved as I deserve. Please.

I signed off my letter to God – or the universe or to whoever the fuck was in charge. I poured my third glass of stolen wine, burnt a stick of incense and read the sacred correspondence out loud to the humid, starry sky. I felt an inner strength and calm I hadn't felt in a while.

The doorbell rang.

I folded the pages in half and rested them on the balcony chair, then walked through the lounge and picked up the intercom handset alongside the front door.

"Hello?"

Darren. He wanted to come in. I dropped the intercom phone and it bounced on its spiral cord. I hesitated, then pushed the button on the receiver and let him in. A few seconds later, he appeared at the front door. He looked like shit. I was silently, smugly, pleased. He was wearing the same clothes as the night before, the same blue-and-silver Black Flys jacket. His pupils were as wide as side plates, his cheeks flushed as though he had been crying. I let him in, wordlessly. He made his way to the lounge and sat on the couch, patting the space next to him by way of invitation.

"I'm sorry," he blubbered. "I felt so shit about what I did to you today and then I ended up seeing Jacques all day and he told me I was a fucking idiot and that you were amazing and I was being a dick for pushing you away ..." He trailed off and rested his head on my shoulder. I instinctively pulled away as though I'd been struck. I still hadn't said a word.

"I know you don't have to forgive me, but what I'm saying is …" He paused and rummaged in his jacket pocket. "Just trust me. Open your mouth."

He deposited a small white pill on my tongue. It was Ecstasy and I swallowed it down with the remainder of my appropriated wine. He took one himself, without any liquid, as was his custom.

"Let's go for a drive," he asked. "Please?"

"Okay." It was the first word I'd uttered since his arrival and my voice sounded strange, detached, not my own.

The drive to Sea Point Promenade was silent. As we drove, he tried to put his hand over mine, but I pulled it away abruptly, staring straight ahead the entire way.

As we pulled up, I came onto the pill. And suddenly I couldn't shut up. We were all eccie-ed up as we sat on the hard, cold wooden bench overlooking the rocks, breathing in the ocean. We spoke for what seemed like hours. He offered me his jacket. It smelled of him and of hope. The stars twinkled and shone brilliantly and, as I struggled to breathe – as I always did on Ecstasy – I wondered if I was breathless from just being with him.

Then he told me he wanted me to be his girlfriend. I was over the fucking crescent moon that shone above us.

Then he told me he was a heroin addict.

I had no idea what that meant. I'd seen *Trainspotting* but that was all I knew about heroin and, to be honest, I hadn't really paid attention to the movie. I genuinely thought my love was bigger than any drug.

I thought I could fix it. I thought I could fix him.

CHAPTER 23

Even Though Everything

Disprin, Panado, Myprodol, Rennie, Sinutab, Alcophyllex, Berocca, Zoloft, Imovane, Dormicum, Physeptone.

It had been two weeks since we had become an 'official' couple. I lined the medication up on the wooden bar counter, smallest to biggest, and wondered which ailments would need to be attended to today: stomach aches, aching muscles, fevers, muscle spasms, tight chests, phlegmy chests, burning lungs, runny nose, migraines, insomnia or fatigue. Or all of the above. I slid the blister pack out of the box of Imovane and pressed one of the tablets out into my hand, then pocketed the little white pill for later. It could be another long, rough night.

I had arrived in Knysna at the dawn of Day Four. My timing could not have been worse. Day Four is notorious as the worst day of heroin withdrawal. My research – if you can call taking one book on heroin users out of the library and reading it while downing two bottles of cheap wine – told me that much. By the time I disembarked from the bus, both Darren and Brad were drowning in excruciating withdrawal symptoms.

Since they had left Cape Town on their mission to get clean

for the first time, I couldn't sleep, I could hardly eat. I couldn't focus on anything. I had told Darren on the phone that I wanted to come. He asked me to come. I didn't need a second invitation. I embezzled an Inter-Cape bus ticket from the travel agency where I worked, told them I had a family emergency to attend to and took the long-ass, smelly trip up the coast, not entirely sure why. I just knew I needed to be there. I'd figure it out when I got there.

Initially, Darren seemed happy to see me but he was withdrawing his *moer* off. Brad, on the other hand, was not thrilled to see me – but he was never happy, even when he was high. His dark brows, which matched his coarse black hair, were always knitted in a scowl irrespective of the occasion. We didn't like each other much. He was the unwanted prophylactic to my burgeoning relationship with Darren. I thought perhaps he felt I was some kind of threat to his friendship, or questioned my motives for wanting to be with his best friend. I hadn't quite worked it out. Despite his obvious disapproval of my presence, I was there for Darren. Fuck Brad.

No, seriously. Fuck him. Fucking junkie.

But now, on the evening of Day Five, withdrawal – and tensions – had eased slightly. Darren was spoon-feeding Brad his nightly dosage of Physeptone with an air of fraternal compassion and medical professionalism. Darren administered his own dose to himself, licking and sucking on the spoon to get the last droplets of the precious liquid. They both helped themselves to a Zoloft, an Imovane and Dormicum, both swallowing the tablets without seeing the need for any liquid.

I'd seen them do this the night before – take these sedatives and sleeping tablets – and the pills had hardly touched sides. It had certainly not lulled either of them to sleep. They were both restless and agitated the entire night, moaning and complaining of a litany of aches and ailments. Darren wouldn't let me near him and had been borderline abusive.

When she found me sobbing uncontrollably in the lounge the night before, Michelle, the glowing hippy-ish blonde whose parents owned the house they were renting, had told me to not take it to heart. She'd offered me a beer from the bar fridge, taken one for herself, sat down on the couch next to me and politely told me to disengage from the situation.

"What the fuck are you doing here?" she sipped her beer slowly, gracefully.

"I don't know." I felt horribly self-conscious next to her, imagining my own pasty skin and listless eyes, and I felt deeply ashamed. "I want to help him."

"How long have you known each other?"

"Four weeks, maybe more." I shrunk back into the sofa, realising the ridiculousness of my answer.

She turned to me, and looked me straight in the eyes. "Honey," she said, "you can't help him. Unless you're prepared to get into one helluva love triangle between you, him and heroin, you have to go. Now."

Bilious anger rose up into my throat and I swallowed it down with a few gulps of beer. She was right, of course, but she didn't understand. I loved him. And he was here, getting clean, and once he did that, it would all be okay. My anxious exploits would not have been in vain. Leaving him now was an unthinkable reality.

When I had finished my drink, Michelle offered me a lift back to Cape Town. "I'm going that way in the next few days anyway. Your call."

We said our goodnights and I made my way back to the bedroom dimly lit by a blue-green lava lamp. I quietly and carefully slipped into bed next to Darren who murmured in his half-sleep and rolled over, enveloping me in his arms. He hadn't touched me, kissed me, showed me any affection, in two days.

He motioned for me to take off my T-shirt and I dutifully obeyed. Clumsily, he tugged my tracksuit pants down over my hips and I pushed them past my knees and pulled them off, kicking them to the floor. We were both in our underwear, closer than we had ever been. I held him in my arms, his head resting on the softness of my naked breasts. His hair was damp with sticky sweat, his skin prickly gooseflesh from the hot-cold fever.

"You've certainly seen me in some compromising positions," his voice was a sweet whisper.

"One or two," I replied, holding him tighter.

"And you're still here?"

"Uh-huh."

I held his gaze but had lost all my words. I wanted to tell him what was so blatantly obvious, but I was not ready to put the enormity of that out there to be mercilessly rejected. We were quiet for a while; he returned his head to my chest and I planted a few small kisses on his clammy forehead.

"Do you love me?" he asked, unexpectedly.

I didn't hesitate. "Yes. Yes, I do."

"Even though...?"

"Even though everything."

CHAPTER 24

It's Always Fun in the Beginning

I was back in Grahamstown, this time taking my much-anticipated pilgrimage with my two friends, Diana and Jax. I had left Darren to fend for himself. The brutal intensity of having a junkie in my life had made me want to escape so badly. So when Diana said she had to go on a media trip to the National Arts Festival, Jax and I decided to take the Translux bus up to join her. We spent suffocating hours in that cramped bus filled with the smell of fried chicken and sweat and stale deodorant and oranges, so were genuinely delighted and grateful to see Diana on the other side.

We spent the next few days bundled up in layers of clothing to fend off the predictable icy July chill, watching theatrical productions during the day to feel cultured and drinking gluhwein in the streets in the evening to get warm and drunk, causing harmless, raucous trouble throughout. We were due to leave the next morning but found ourselves at a makeshift club somewhere in the middle of the town to celebrate the end of our trip.

And now it appeared we were about to embark on another one. Palm outstretched, I reached over to accept the tiny black microdot. I looked around to see if anyone was observing the exchange but the motley collection of festival revellers gathered around the rooftop fire pit could not have seemed less interested in what I was doing.

I glanced down at my nonexistent watch and worked out the imaginary hours we still had before we left. It seemed vaguely sufficient. Diana and I locked eyes – eyes gleaming with shared recklessness, excitement and fear of the unknown – and then I downed the minuscule tablet with a swig of my cider.

The time that passed waiting to determine whether the drug actually worked was interminable. It took exactly one and half vodka-lime-and-sodas before it became difficult for me to swallow my own saliva and for a warm, snaking pressure to make itself known up and down my vertebrae.

It had begun.

Diana and I looked at each other simultaneously and both grinned broadly. She reached for my hand and gave it a comforting squeeze. I returned it in equal pressure and then let go, though I didn't want to. I looked around. My vision had become definitively warped and brighter around the edges and everything appeared to have developed a silver-white aura. Noises were beginning to distort and sounded both near and far away at the same time. I felt my heart beating in my dry throat. I took a sip from my drink, but even getting the glass to my lips was an ordeal. It was almost impossible to swallow.

Oh my dear God, my body was no longer functioning!

I looked down at my hand. It looked abnormally large, I could clearly see every pore, every groove, every line. Slowly, I stretched out my fingers, then balled them up to make a fist.

Okay, oooooookay. I hadn't gone lame. I would try this again.

I brought the glass to my lips, took another sip, swirled the cold liquid around in my mouth and willed myself to swallow it. I did.

Thank God. I was fine. Utterly fucked out of my bracket, but otherwise fine.

The repetitive bassy beat of the music travelled up my spine. I hadn't heard the song before but the lyrics were so familiar.

Holy fuckballs! Was that my name in that song?

"Diana!" I turned and tapped her on the shoulder, "Can you hear this song? Is it saying my name?"

She was engaged in a deep conversation with a tall, young moustachioed man in a multicoloured poncho and no shoes. She looked at me as though I were mad, then the look changed to one of compassion – compassion for the mad.

"Oh my darling, you're tripping your tits off. I really don't think so."

I tried to separate the discordance of sounds in my mind, but still a titanium ocean filled with copper cymbals was crashing against metal trashcans in my brain. It sounded like a sweet, chaotic orchestra. I saw myself playing percussion.

Desiree, come on down. Desiree, come on down …

Goddammnit! The song was actually calling me by my name. My entire, now pulsating body felt drawn to the dance floor to find out who or what was calling me. I pushed myself up off the cement seat and, although unsteady on my feet at first, eventually mastered the art of walking like a quasi-normal person. I focused my energy on looking like I was not intoxicated to the gills, smoothing down my clothes and fluffing out my curls. I felt a tightness in my face and realised I was sucking in my cheeks and moving my lips like a fish. I put a stop to that. The room wasn't so much spinning as it was tilting at an angle, making all of my attempts at maintaining some semblance of normalcy that much more difficult. I wondered how people and objects weren't sliding right off the rooftop …

I needed to confront that DJ. I took the stairs to the level below and at the base merged immediately into the smoky, heaving dance floor. I rubbed my eyes and my ears popped. The same song pumped insistently through the speakers and now, closer to the source, I was beyond convinced; the vocals had been inviting me to be exactly where I was at that very moment. I peered through the pink-grey smoke, searching for the DJ booth, and it suddenly appeared next to me, on my right. I hung my fingertips on the edge of the cubicle and stood on tiptoes to catch a glimpse of the offending purveyor of music.

Oh, my sweet fuck! It was Gary. Gary Mason!

I knew him. He was one of Darren's best friends. I could ask him. I *had* to know. I moved closer to the side entrance of the booth to catch his attention and waved. He glanced up, in between mixing, smiled and waved back in recognition. I motioned to him that I wanted to come behind the decks and he waved me up. We hugged and he kissed me on the cheek, which burned hot on my skin. I waited until the song was done and he had mixed in another track before tackling him.

I cleared my throat, wondering if I was still able to speak English. "Gary, that song ..."

"What song, darlin'?" His thick Irish accent reverberated right through me. I felt instantly aroused.

"The one before. Did it have my name in it? Did it says, '*Desiree, come on down*'?"

He laughed. He put his lips to my ear so he could be heard over the noise. "Ah, darlin', if ye heard yer name, then ye heard yer name."

"Don't fuck with me, Mason. It's driving me mad."

"Ye're here, aren't ye? The song got ye here."

He replaced his headphones over his ears and gave me a squeeze on the shoulder that I felt right down in my ankles.

I stepped down from the booth and took my place in front of it. Then I danced, ripped apart by the bass and treble and beat and vocals of a series of mystical and mind-numbing tracks. I smiled. It was good. So, so, so fucking good.

I would have, could have danced forever had I not felt an almost violent tug at my arm. It was Diana, concern and disapproval in her eyes. Jax stood next to her, grimacing like a sibling silently warning another that they were in deep, deep shit.

"Where the fuck have you been?" Diana demanded, rocking slightly.

"I've been dancing. I just got here."

"Fuck's sake. You just disappeared. You've been gone for ages. We've been looking for you everywhere."

"Ages?"

"Yes, ages. We're leaving. Here's your bag. Let's go."

As we exited the club, I saw the horizon crack open and streaks of silver-yellow sunlight escape the skyline.

Oh, fuck.

We had horribly mistimed our little escapade. It was already dawn and we had only just begun.

"I'm hungry."

"Me too."

"I couldn't possibly eat right now."

I unzipped my sling bag, removed my lip gloss from the inside pocket and took the cap off – and, immediately horrified by the colour and texture, returned the offending make-up to my bag. I licked my lips. They tasted like cold metal and felt like warm rubber.

"You see that?" asked Diana. "Over there ... I think it's a Debonairs."

I shuffled my bum over to the space between the driver and passenger's seats and squinted at the distance.

"Pizza? Really?"

Diana took a swig from her bottle of vodka-laced soda water. "I'm on hold."

I could hear the tinny, tinkly hold music like teeny little forks stabbing at my cerebral cortex.

"Yes, directory enquiries? I'm looking for the number of the Debonairs Pizza place you can see from the Botanical Gardens ..." She was clearly irritated by whoever was on the other end. "I don't know *where*! Oh, the town? Grahamstown. Yes, pizza ..."

I lay back down across the back seat and swallowed hard. My flesh felt like it was living independently of my bones. The edges of my teeth sharp on my tongue, into which I'd already chewed multiple little holes. And everything was just so fucking bright.

It was 9.58 am.

We were parked in the northern parking lot of the Grahamstown Botanical Gardens, under the shade of some nondescript, but noisy, trees. We were supposed to be on our way back to Cape Town, but that was obviously not happening. Diana and Jax were sitting up front arranging for a pizza to be delivered to the car at 10 in the morning and I was lying in the back wondering about the evolutionary necessity of facial hair, especially on women. I stretched and reached to turn the window winder. I needed air.

"We really getting pizza?" I asked.

"Yes, of course," came Jax's decisive response. "I'm starving."

"I can't eat when I'm tripping," I whined.

"You'll want to when it gets here," Diana assured me.

"As long as there's no fruit on the pizza," I insisted.

"It's ham and pineapple."

"Fuck, no."

"We asked you what you wanted," said Diana, "but you were … er … busy."

"Warm fruit on pizza? Really?" I said, with very real disgust. "I'm going to go get some fresh air." I sat up and swung the backdoor open.

"Don't go far," heeded Jax.

"And don't talk to strangers. Or ghosts," added Diana.

I wandered away from the car but could still hear their melodic dialogue. The light was so fucking bright and I cursed the loss of my sunglasses at some point along the journey. I did 'tracers', making arcs in the air with my hands, and watched the trail of psychedelic sparkles that followed my fingertips. I was definitely still tripping balls. I found a path leading off the parking lot, not too far from the car, and I was about to step onto it when the noise started. A loud *chop-chop-choppy* sound of what could only be large blades slicing through the air accompanied by the whirring noise of an engine. Then it was just there, descending slowly from the heavens, landing in the clearing next to the parking lot, a shiny red-and-white helicopter, propellers spinning, engine whirring furiously. I stood rooted to the spot, completely overwhelmed. Was it all just a hallucination?

Jax and Diana were suddenly by my side, one with hands on hips, the other bent over at the waist, both laughing maniacally.

"Pizza's here!" they shouted in unison.

Yes, the helicopter was very real – a fire-fighting chopper

coming to refill at the nearby dam – but, no, it was not delivering pizza. A very confused delivery guy *really* did that a few minutes later, right to the car. We ate it on the bonnet of the car, those trees crashing ominously above us, me picking off the pineapple pieces and tossing them into the nearby bushes.

Best. Pizza. Ever.

Best times ever. But that was all about to change.

CHAPTER 25

Surrender

There was blood on the comforter. Darren's blood from the syringe he had used to inject heroin for the first time.

"This feels ... amazing ..." His words drifted away, as he stretched his long, heavy frame back on the futon.

The comforter had been a gift from my mother; I would never have chosen it for myself. Completely ineffective in the role for which it was designed. Too hot for that sweltering summer in January; and never so cold that it provided any comfort. It was white with a blue-and-yellow network of linear shapes, lines and squares. I could never work out the pattern it followed, though I knew one existed; so busy that if I stared at it too long and then looked quickly at the grey-white bedroom wall, the image would remain, floating about a ruler's length away from my eyes. The yellow was too yellow, a processed margarine kind of yellow and the blue was just too blue. Too blue, too yellow. Too cheerful. But that day another colour joined and disturbed the dizzying motif: red. Blood red. Actual blood. Darren's blood from the hypodermic needle. A few crimson drops now blackening in that stifling heat in my small bedroom. A dark, sickening, vampire-like urge rose up in me, mixing with the utter disbelief.

As he stretched out, the empty syringe dropped next to me where I perched on the frame of the futon, watchfully. I couldn't speak. I wanted to scream. Instead, I hugged my knees and rocked slightly. It wasn't supposed to be like this. It wasn't supposed to have progressed from snorting and chasing to spiking. I was supposed to have gotten him clean. But nine months later and it had only gotten worse. He had returned from that detox in Knysna and gone straight to score. The last several months had been a vicious cycle of more sweaty, failed detoxes, weepy apologies, empty promises and unstoppable using. I had found myself doing things I had not thought myself capable of, but they all came so naturally to me: stealing money from work, manipulating and lying to family and friends to extort cash from them, taking out an overdraft on my bank account and spending it on drugs. All of it was to support *his* habit. We were either perpetually scoring in Mowbray or buying bottles of Subutex and boxes of Dormicum from some dodgy pharmacy, obtained from scripts scrawled out by the even more shady ask-no-questions psychiatrist in Constantia.

I was also still shovelling cocaine up my nose and washing pills down my throat at any given opportunity. I was still going to clubs and parties with Diana and staying awake for entire weekends and using my own drugs of sweet choice to mask my confusion and pain. I still pretended to the outside world that everything was okay. He was the DJ and I was his girlfriend. I suspected people knew about his addiction but no one said a word, at least not to me. Darren and I argued about it often but I invariably collapsed into submission. He threatened to leave if I couldn't accept that he was what he was. I couldn't entertain that notion, him leaving, so I did what I needed to do to make him stay. We were co-conspirators in a dangerous lie. I really had tried so fucking hard. And the fucker kept using up all my tinfoil.

Hot, heavy tears of frustration sprang up in my eyes. Every time, every single time, he tried to get clean, I really believed it would work. I felt so sick and so in love. I knew that I loved him. I knew that he loved what he called "his medicine". It was a sickening cycle of obsession and lies and misplaced hope. Now he looked so peaceful. I picked up the hypodermic needle and, resting it on my upturned palm, presented it to him.

"Here …" I said, "show me how."

CHAPTER 26

Clucking

I stretched out my legs. The numb ache in my shins was unsoothable and unreachable. I scratched my right thigh and the itch migrated to my protruding hipbone, then to my stomach.

I itched all over.

I lay curled up on the couch in a near-foetal position, in my panties and a too-small T-shirt. Prickly gooseflesh and cold, clammy perspiration covering the surface of my skin.

Hot. Cold. Hot and cold.

I stretched my legs again and the muscles in my calves resisted, aching rebelliously. I reached down and tried to knead out the knotted ball of muscle but I knew it was futile. The pain was so elusive, deeply entrenched in parts of my body that could not be touched. In my bones, in my teeth, in my very breath.

I was in full-blown withdrawal.

The daylight threatened to wind its way in through a tear in the dusty purple curtain. I had no idea what time it was. Mid-morning? He'd been gone for ages. More than three increments of 20 minutes, which was how we seemed to measure time these days. I prayed silently for his return. It was the only time I ever took advantage of sweet baby Jesus's mercy and unconditional grace: when I needed a fix.

Which was daily, every four hours at best now.

I knew it was Saturday because I had been at work the day before. I had landed a job at a prestigious public relations agency a few months after we met, but before I had given myself over entirely to the sweet evil. I was employed as the receptionist but within four weeks they had promoted me to an accounts assistant. The co-director, a force to be reckoned with in the PR world, recognised my potential and bumped me upstairs, quite literally, to work alongside and be mentored by accounts executives and, of course, herself.

I was exceptional at what I did. I was a fast learner, absorbing skills and knowledge like a sponge, and using my natural autodidactic abilities to pretend that I was capable of anything they asked. I was teachable and compliant and dripped with politeness and respect. I was employee-of-the-fucking month, if not only in my own head. But, as good as I was at my job, I was even better at hiding what I did after the computers were shut down, the office doors had been locked and I went home to Darren. In the beginning it was hiding cocaine-binge hangovers on Monday mornings or sometimes Thursday mornings, depending on how successful the week had been. I made instant friends with a colleague, Louisa, and our shared love for cocaine, wine and talking shit until 3 am created a conspiratorial bond. One midweek night we were working on an account in Stellenbosch and slept over at their hotel; we drove all the way to town to score and then hid our delicious indiscretion behind dark sunglasses and forced smiles at the staff year-end lunch at some fancy restaurant in Franschhoek where neither of us could stomach the food or bear the December sunshine and heat trapped in the lush valley.

We laughed all the way home, down the N2, blurry-eyed and victorious from having successfully pulled the wool over everyone's eyes, vowing never to do that again ... and then made plans to meet up on the weekend to do it all over again.

Once I started using heroin, all other drugs took a back seat. I no longer sought the hyperactive, driven, arrogant effect of uppers. I demanded the beautiful numbness, the comatose calm I had finally found. Nothing that had come before it brought such emotional anaesthesia, so I was committed. I was a card-carrying, one-narcotic woman.

Being a full-time junkie meant that I had to up my game of a double life considerably. I had more to hide. I had more to lose: heroin, Darren, my job – in that order. At the time, I truly believed Darren was the pinnacle of my personal Maslow's hierarchy of needs. I couldn't live without him. I couldn't imagine a world in which that was even a remote possibility. I also couldn't live without heroin. It was a treacherous twin coupling but I thought I might physically die without my lethal, codependent craziness.

Darren was also the one who scored for us. I would be the one who devised plans to get our hands on money or it would be a collaborative criminal effort. But he always scored. I was veritable junkie royalty, having my drug procured and delivered to me every day, even at work where I would be withdrawing deliriously, clenching my teeth to form a passable smile. Waiting, waiting for his message or his call that he had been successful and was waiting in the driveway of the apartment block next door to our offices. I would slip out of the office, dash to the car, kiss him sincerely and gratefully, and then rush back to the agency's toilet to shoot up. My smile wouldn't be as forced, as contrived, after that.

The lies and manipulation would slip effortlessly from my lips. At one point, I had the entire office feeling sorry for me for my litany of make-believe ailments and my bravery at having overcome them in the face of such adversity. I had become a heartless junkie, twisting the entire world with deceitful words to fulfil my narcotic needs.

While Darren was the heroin hunter-gatherer, I wasn't much of a forager at all. But we worked tirelessly at perfecting our habit as though our lives depended on it – which it did on so many precarious levels.

He'd been gone for fucking ages now. I needed water, but it seemed an impossibly far journey to the kitchen. Well over six metres away. My eyes scanned the empty spaces where kitchen appliances used to be: the washing machine, microwave, dishwasher, even the toaster. All had found their way to 'Crack Converters' during times of sheer desperation. Always with the intention of buying them back, of course, but that very rarely happened any more. Desperation was our default setting.

I heard the metallic click of the key in the front door and a chill of relief rushed through my veins. But another voice, not just his, travelled in distorted waves down the passage. An unfamiliar voice. I grabbed the oversized nylon jacket slung over the couch and pulled it up over my body. I was hidden from sight in the same way a toddler covers their eyes when they play hide-and-seek. Sweat droplets rolled down my nose and onto my cracked lips and I licked thirstily at the sticky, salty liquid.

I tracked the muffled sound of the stranger's movement. They were in the front room. You could call it a lounge but no one had visited in over a year. They were moving something. The armchair? Dragging, scraping sounds across the wooden floors. No, it was the antique sideboard his grandmother had given to us.

"I'll give you R400 for it," a gruff, British-accented voice offered. I thought about William, how I loved the sweet sound of his voice. How, if I had stayed with him, I probably wouldn't be hiding under a jacket about to crap myself or vomit.

"It's worth much more," came Darren's hopeful reply, jolting me out of my hopeful reverie.

"No one else will take it. Four hundred, that's it."

A resigned sigh. Negotiation over. "Okay. I'll help you load it onto the bakkie."

More dragging noises mixed with the delicate tinkling of the ornate glass panels against the heavy oak shelves. The front door shut with a thud and the noises trailed off into the street.

Four hundred. Eight quarters of heroin.

We would be okay for another day.

CHAPTER 27

The Psychic, the Addict and the Englishman

William stood in front of me like some kind of apparition. We had arranged to meet at Oak Lodge, a backpackers where he was staying in town. Darren had been unhappy about this arrangement – vocally so.

"Why the fuck do you need to see your ex?" he demanded.

"For closure."

"Fuck closure!" He was pacing up and down in a room so small that it couldn't really be paced. Two steps, turn. Two steps, turn. "I'm taking you there." I felt like an alacritous hostage but agreed.

But there was no closure happening at the hostel where we arranged to meet. William was asking me to go back to England with him. I was dumbfounded and high, not an ideal combination for making a life-changing decision.

"You're too late." I was angry. I perched on the end of an over-used sun lounger, trying very hard to keep some distance between us. He was blonder and more tanned, healthy, even by the half-light of the poolside globes and the full moon.

"Baby," he explained emphatically, "there was nothing I could do about the situation. That's just the way the overland tours work. But I'm here now." He took a tentative step towards me and I didn't stop him.

"It's April," I continued. "You were supposed to be here in December." My voice was raised and shaky.

"I told you that was impossible. I was in the middle of Africa. And, anyway, I've been leaving messages with your folks for over a week to say I'd be arriving."

I had been holed up with Darren in his parents' townhouse in Milnerton for a week, doing heroin and growing like fungi in the dark. I had been entirely uncontactable. It was only a spontaneous and rare call to my mother that had revealed William was in town and looking for me.

My heart was racing, my chest almost caving in on itself. I was still in love with him. He was "the light-haired man".

Just a few weeks back I had been to the Obz Holistic Fair with a dear friend and, not taking it too seriously, paid a tired-looking psychic in the corner of the community hall 50 bucks to tell me the obvious.

"You're going to have to make a life-altering decision," she whispered in her croaky, two-packs-a-day voice.

Don't I always, I thought, cynically.

She disregarded my jaded retort and continued: "Soon you will have to choose between a dark-haired man and light-haired man. That decision will change everything."

I was intrigued, but couldn't access who the light-haired man could be. Darren was obviously the dark-haired man. He consumed my every thought. William, though, had been evicted from my mind, relegated to a pile of raging resentment and deep disappointment.

"Who is the light-haired man?" I had asked, trying not to seem too intrigued.

I checked in my sling bag but was out of cash. "Thanks," I lied. "That's all I need to know."

And here it was manifested: the light-haired man was offering me an out. He was offering to pay for my ticket back to England, to an old, safe, familiar life.

"I love you …" He was now less than a metre away. I wanted to reach out and touch him, make sure he was real. I wanted him to hold me and put the shattered shards back together again the way he had always done in the past.

I bit my bottom lip so as not to respond. I did still love him. He had been The One before The Other One had come along. I knew I was making a massive mistake. I knew this decision would cement the fact that there would be no going back. I knew I was saying no to a life that I really wanted, a man I desperately needed.

"I can't, Will," I stood up, tears starting to well in my eyes. "I'm in a relationship now." With a junkie. My entire existence is a shithole. I think I have a drug problem. I think I have a serious, deadly life problem.

I dug my hand into the pocket of my denim jacket to find a tissue. My hand found the letter I had written months before to God. How the fuck had that got there? I felt a strong, insistent urge to show William the letter, tell him that I was sorry and that he was The One. That *he* was my Big Love. Instead, I stuffed it further down into the pocket.

Save me, I wanted to say. *Please save me.*

But those words failed to find the cold, crisp air.

"One last kiss goodbye then?" he ventured.

He was right next to me, his face radiating the warmth from layers of sunburn and forgiveness and love. But he was giving up and I was letting him. If I kissed him, I knew I would never leave him and I had made an earnest promise to Darren to stay with him no matter what. Darren would change. He would get clean. *We* would get clean. It would happen. We would be happy.

"I can't," I pushed passed him. "I have to go. Bye."

I left William standing at the poolside. I half-ran through the noisy backpackers, trying to find the exit. It smelled of weed and sun cream and freedom. My life smelled of heroin simmering in a dirty spoon.

I found the front door and, wiping my tears from my cheeks

with the back of my hand, made my way to the dark-haired man, the junkie, to Darren, who was waiting in the car outside, the engine still running.

CHAPTER 28

Butterfly Kisses

"Just close all the windows and curtains!"

"Why are you carrying a till?"

"Just do it!" he yelled, dropping the cash register on the terra-cotta tiled kitchen counter, cracking part of the surface. "And switch off all the lights."

"We don't have electricity. It ran out this morning." Darren turned at me accusingly as though I had personally sucked all the electricity out of the box fixed to the wall.

"I gave you money!" he was still yelling. I stood cemented to the floor in the middle of the lounge, watching him stride up and down like a predatory pack animal.

I knew what was to come.

He walked over to the window and peeked out through the slit between the two drops of old, purple curtaining. As he yanked them closed, the curtain rail dislodged from the wall, pulling a small chunk of plaster and wall with it. When Darren was angry, his rage was primal and took up all the space in the room, pushing everyone and everything up against the walls in trepidation of what was to come. What always came.

"Why're you back so early?" I ventured, almost whispering. "You were supposed to be gone for two weeks."

"It's all fucked up, it's all fucked up." He flopped down on the stained couch, cigarette burns dotting the upholstery – some accidentally, some done on purpose, like the smiley face I had burned into the armrest while watching CNN on repeat cycle for hours one night. He buried his face in his hands, then ran them through his hair, tugging at the ends. He repeated this action, wincing with pain a few times.

I knew what was to come. What always came.

"Baby, what happened?" I asked, picking up the vibration of his rage and panic from where I stood. "And where's Cliff?"

I didn't actually give a fuck where Cliff was, that racist cunt, but they had left together two days ago, Cliff with a master plan in his bigoted brain that involved them driving up to Knysna. I wasn't privy to the rest of the plan, but there would be money and drugs at the end of the 10-day sojourn and that was all I needed to know. I was also relieved that it didn't involve me; not like the attempted armed robbery in the Northern Suburbs, with me delegated the role of the sweaty-palmed getaway driver. That time it was the idea of a small-time dealer, Jackson. He had heard about a house in which there was reportedly a safe that held masses of cash, firearms and jewellery. Jackson also had a gun. I hated guns; they scared the shit out of me every time he brought them into the house. Darren made me hold the gun, point and go through the motions of firing even though it wasn't loaded. It was far heavier than I had anticipated and the cold metal singed the palms of my hand. Shaking almost uncontrollably, I aimed it at the passage wall, cocked it and squeezed the trigger with great difficulty, eventually resorting to both my index fingers. The firearm and I fell to the floor, both men laughing at my incompetence in violence.

"She can't make bang-bang," Jackson sniggered, retrieving the gun from the wood floor where it had made a dent in one of the floorboards. No one retrieved me from the floor.

All Darren and I needed to do was provide the angle grinder to access the safe and the car. It was ridiculous, asking two junkies to organise a crime of that scale. It felt like an elaborate practical joke. We kept putting the angle grinder on buy-back at Cash Converters to get money to score and Jackson would arrive and we would be high with no angle grinder and no petrol in the car. Not exactly Crime-of-the-Century conditions. One day we actually did manage to get our shit together. We piled into the rusty, dented, teal Opel Corsa completely out of our criminal depth and off our heads on heroin. Except for Jackson who did a fat line of fluffy cocaine right off our cluttered kitchen counter, pushing aside piles of dirty plates and dishes and wiping a section clean with an even grimier dishtowel. He was a drug dealer and criminal, but I could tell that he judged me, that he thought we were trash.

Darren and Jackson were wearing matching blue overalls procured from Jackson's friends who worked at a car wash. The plan was that they were going to claim to be from Telkom and they were checking a fault in the landlines of houses in the area. They needed a white guy to gain access because no one would just let a Nigerian in. That would be insanity. But everyone trusted a good-looking white guy with a smile that oozed charm and eyes that spoke of trust, even if they were cross-eyed from nodding in and out of intoxicated consciousness. I had even designed and printed fake documents at work to back up their story. I sat in the baking-hot car in the street diagonally across from the house. I was shaking from oncoming cold turkey. I gripped the steering wheel to steady myself, constantly checking whether my feet could reach the pedals. The sweat dripped from my forehead into my eyes; I refused to wind down the window to let the afternoon summer heat out of the stifling car. I kept my eyes fixed on the house, waiting. Waiting.

I watched them emerge from the front gate. They did not seem to be in any particular hurry. Darren walked up to the driver's side, sweat pouring down from his temples.

"Get out, baby, I'll drive."

It had been a monumental failure. They had gained access to the house. A middle-aged Indian woman and what appeared to be her elderly mother were at home and bought into Darren and Jackson's story without hesitation. They went around the house pretending to fix telephone jacks. They even found the room with the magical safe. But when it came to executing the plan, they couldn't. They didn't. Their fear, consciences and lack of experience won over and they thanked the house's inhabitants and left. We drove straight to Cash Converters and pawned the angle grinder; no buy-back.

The Knysna plan, however, had seemed like a sure thing ... but here he was, two days later back home, frenetic and paranoid. He walked to the bedroom. I followed a few paces behind. I knew what was going to come next.

"Where's the *goed*?" He was searching under the pile of clothes in the cupboard where we usually kept any drugs.

I knew what was to come.

My voice was lost in the turmoil and fear churning in my stomach. I wanted to vomit.

He had organised four grams – two for me, to see me through the 10 days he would be gone. Abdul had even given us an extra quarter on account of our bulk purchase. I had held the plastic-wrapped treasures in my hand all the way home from Mowbray, smiling, feeling as though I was set for life.

I had been *so good* on the first day when Darren had departed with Cliff. I had gone to work and only used two quarters. But Friday night had been another story. I had sat in bed, duvet drawn over my knees, plastic teardrops of smack lined up on the side table next to the bed, alongside my syringe and charred spoon, and had started rereading one of my favourite books, *To Kill A Mockingbird*. And then, in between reading and smoking cigarettes, I shot up, half a quarter at a time, for the whole night until the sun rose unexpectedly, those fucking annoying morning birds chirping their beaks off. By dawn I had finished the book. I wanted to call my daughter Scout. Or Harper. I had also finished all the heroin. I had injected nearly two grams into my brittle body in succession. I hadn't cared if I overdosed. I hadn't cared if I lived or died, the latter being the preferable option if I had to choose. There would have been no one to help revive me or call for assistance. My phone was also in the *pun*, as it was every weekend. I had used 10 days' worth of heroin in a few long, opioid-drenched hours, and now Darren was looking for it.

"Where is it?" he demanded, turning to me. He had tossed all of the clothes out of the cupboard and I knew that's where they'd stay for days, maybe weeks.

I sat on the bed, face drawn to my heaving chest. He lifted my chin up with one finger, forcing me to lock eyes with him.

"Where.The.Fuck.Is.The.Smack?" he growled.

"I used it all."

He swung his arm back and punched me in the face. Other men had smacked me around a few times before but Darren had never laid a finger on me so the force of his knuckles connecting with my cheekbone and eye socket was an entirely new kind of anguish. My head snapped back to the left and then forward again but, apart from that involuntary reaction, I didn't move. A searing agony radiated through my skull and tears immediately streamed down my face. My hands were still on my lap, shaking, like the rest of my body. My mind went numb and I fell mute.

I knew this would happen.

"You stupid *poes*," he spat, grabbing a jacket from the pile on the floor. He stormed out the room and stomped down the passage, yanked open the front door and slammed it behind him with such force that the house shook, dust shimmying from the ceiling and down the walls. I walked over to the frameless mirror leaning against the bedroom wall and raised my hand to my cheek. It was tender and distended. My eye was swelling shut, the flesh tinged blue-purple.

He was right. I was a stupid *poes*. I'd deserved that.

CHAPTER 29

A Matter of Economics

It was a sordid courtship structured purely along economical lines. Supply and demand. I needed heroin; Abdul, my dealer, wanted sex. I had exhausted all other anxious options, all other possible means. I could find nothing to pawn or exchange. I was too feeble to steal anything. All I had left to bargain with was my vagina.

Darren and I had been separated for three months, a violent and bloody amputation performed with a blunt steak knife. The cops had come all the way from Knysna and he was arrested for stealing the cash register, and then sent to rehab. After he left, I had been ferried off to a dodgy rehab in Piketberg. I was soon evicted under a cloud of disgrace for fucking one of the inmates because I thought he would give me drugs. I had tried staying at my dad's flat in Diep River but that only lasted a few weeks. His new girlfriend, four years younger than me and twice my height, favoured tik. Our drugs of choice clashed as heavily as our personalities. I *skarelled* and smoked meth with her for a while, but when she started stealing my mother's old crockery, pots and dinner services to sell for drugs I had an out-of-place pang of conscience. When she blamed it on me, pulling the proverbial wool over my dad's eyes, my mother took me in. Reluctantly.

Every morning, my mother locked me in. She would close the door behind her, turn the key – *click* – in the lock and leave for work. I would then set to work … I would open up the flat-facing side of the tiny double trapdoor in the kitchen wall intended for rubbish collection by Thomas, the superintendent, and wait to hear the telltale noises of him collecting the metal bin through the passage-facing door. I would run to the kitchen and poke my head through the opening.

"Please leave it unlocked," I'd smile as charmingly as one withdrawing from heroin could. This was our daily ritual, Thomas's and mine. He would leave the latch off the hook and, once I was ready, I'd run to the intercom at the front door to buzz the driveway gate open, run back to the kitchen, toss my backpack through the rubbish chute, squeeze myself through and scuttle down three flights of stairs to make it out onto the road before the double gate shut with a decisive clang. I would return the same way I left before my mother returned home from work every evening. And every evening she would walk past the trap door in the corridor and slide the hook over the metal hole, muttering about how Thomas always left it open.

I had finally lost my job at the PR agency where I'd led my dubious double life for close on four years. I had lost another job after that because of theft. I was unemployable but I wasn't too upset. Work got in the way of my using so it suited me just fine. I would spend my days lying, cheating, stealing, bargaining, defrauding, anything I needed to in order to get my fix.

But today was different.

Abdul drove the Red Citi Golf down to the river. Two large bushes off the dirt track created a hideaway of sorts, obscured from the passing traffic hurtling down the freeway. The heat of the day and the withdrawal meant that I was sweating so profusely that the back of my thighs stuck to the vinyl seat. The solidity of my denial dictated that I should, at the very least, go through the motions of more traditional and acceptable foreplay.

"I didn't know you liked me like that," I smiled coquettishly up at him from under my damp eyelids. He frowned. His black skin shone with sweat. He smelled of it too; musky, manly, overwhelming.

I needed to use first, to be outside of my body while he was inside of it.

"Can I have the quarter please?" He retrieved the plastic teardrop from the car's ashtray and handed it to me. I grabbed at it and he held it just out of reach.

"Sex first," his tone was firm. It was non-negotiable. He was having no part of my delusional courtship ritual. He motioned for me to move over to the back seat of the car.

"Do you have a condom?" Not that I cared, but it seemed as though I should. In a former life, that would have been the next obvious question. He frowned again and dismissed my request without a word.

Awkwardly, I clambered over the passenger seat and lay down across the back. My neck rested uncomfortably on the armrest on the back door, the window winder jabbing into the back of my skull. I unbuttoned my shorts and pushed them down over my ankles. Panties next. I waited, exposed, as he climbed into the back of the car and fell on top of and then into me. His shoulder pummelled up against my jaw, shoving my head further into the hard knob of the window winder. I wanted to scream. I wanted to bite a chunk of his flesh out of his shoulder. Vomit rose up from my stomach and I gagged, then swallowed hard. I closed my eyes and imagined a younger version of myself admonishing me for taking things this far.

It was over. He was spent, his full dead weight crushing my protruding hipbones and ribcage. I felt the wetness leak slowly down my thighs. Everything smelled of sex tinged with subtle violence.

The sickening withdrawal was making me hallucinate. I saw a much younger version of myself, probably four or five years old, sitting in the front passenger seat, staring back at me. Her eyes were big and wide, but the rest of her face was expressionless. She shook her head slowly, from side to side, disapprovingly, then placed her index finger to her lips: yet again a silent witness to a new, horrific secret. I shut my eyes tightly then soundlessly told her to grow the fuck up.

This was how things were in the real world. I was a whore now.

* * *

Fuck.

I grabbed the tip of the thin metal between the edge of my front top and bottom teeth and drew it out of my skin. The needle had broken off in an already hardening vein and the syringe was still full of hot liquid heroin. I hadn't even shot up yet.

Fuck, fuck, fuck.

I chucked the rest of my dirty works into my small, frayed backpack and carefully laid the syringe in the inside side pocket, careful not to push the plunger against the side of the bag. I had no money for syringes and that fucking, self-righteous whore at the pharmacy on the corner was starting to eye me suspiciously when I asked for insulin syringes. She had even had the audacity to ask me what kind of insulin I used but I had googled the names of insulin types at the internet café when my mom had given me money to go search for a job, so I was able to rattle off the answer the pharmacist wanted to hear. It didn't make sense that a pharmacy so close to an intravenous drug hub would not have the foresight to just sell us fucking clean needles: no questions asked.

Smug cunts.

I exited the public bathroom stall and made my way to the perimeter of the taxi rank. I would need to find someone with needles. I would need to find Eugene.

I wasn't entirely sure of his background. Mid-thirties probably, but he looked much younger. I was convinced heroin was some sort of age-defying preservative. Everyone I knew who used it looked much younger than their chronological age. I knew Eugene came from a well-to-do-family and that at one point he had worked at a bank and had been fired for theft. Our histories weren't important though. Our comradeship rested on our mutual desire for and the use of drugs. That was all there was to know. And that Eugene never tried to extract sexual favours from me. Being gay – though never admitting it – may have been a contributing factor. I suspected he, like I, sold his sex for drugs. Quite possibly to the same men.

I walked up the embankment to the subway and then down the stairs, automatically blocking my nose against the pervasive stench of urine that permanently saturated it. I had one piece of scrawled street art memorised word for word as I had spent a night trying to sleep in that tunnel, staring at it: "Every night I flood my bed with tears, my eyes grow weak with sorrow and they fail because of my foes." The message held meaning of sorts and it was comforting to see it every time I crossed under that subway. Slowly, I climbed the stairs to the other side. My legs were heavy and cramping. Eugene was always loitering around the Main Road side of the tracks. I crossed the vast bus terminus, which hung heavy with noxious petrol fumes, filled with frustrated afternoon passengers already forming dense lines alongside the buses, and headed in the direction of the bar, Champs.

Eugene – dressed in camo pants, a torn, dark, dirty blue jersey and sneakers that had once been white – was outside, literally wrapped around a lamppost. His curly hair and cocoa skin were shiny with oil. I wasn't sure if he was high or withdrawing.

"Hey Eugene," I waved, trembling slightly as the tremors washed through me.

"Miss D!" he greeted, jovially. He was high.

"I need some help please." I leaned in and whispered, "My needle broke."

He looked at me thoughtfully. "Come ... this way," he said, leading me into the notorious bar. It was a complete dive: the stench of old, stale booze and second-hand smoke. The half-linoleum half-carpeted floor was sticky with what was probably a combination of spilled alcohol and vomit. It was occupied by the unemployed, alcoholics and daytime drinkers, all lined up at the bar on elevated stools. The TV was mounted high up on a wall behind a padlocked metal cage, showing the latest sporting event: horse racing. I thought briefly of my dad, then shook the memory away. No time for sentimentality. We pushed our way through saloon-style swing doors – one hanging precariously from two hinges – into the bathroom stall and sat down on the grimy, tiled floor. I withdrew my full but broken syringe, and he withdrew his own hypodermic needle and spoon.

He squirted the mixture from my broken syringe into the spoon, heated the mixture up with the flame of his smiley-face Clipper lighter and then expertly drew it up into his own syringe. I pumped my left fist multiple times and identified a vein at the back of my hand. The veins in the crook of my elbow had long ago hardened and calcified.

"Don't forget, my dear, sharing is caring," he warned, melodically.

I inserted the tip of the needle into my skin, found the vein, drew the plunger back and, with a gratified smile, watched my own blood mix with the heroin. I loved that part of shooting up: seeing the two fluids mix; my bright red blood becoming one with my precious smack. I waited a few seconds, then eased the plunger forward, pushing most of the liquid into my beckoning system. The sweet respite was almost instantaneous. I leaned back against the stall door. I drew the needle out of the back of my hand and handed it to Eugene.

He looked at me solemnly. "Miss D ... you don't have the AIDS, do you?"

I laughed through my beautiful high. There was an insistent knock on the toilet door.

"No, Genie."

He got up on his haunches, pulling himself up to the basin. "Just in case," he said. He twisted open the tap and held the tip of the needle under hot water for a few seconds. I laughed, amused, again. "You know that doesn't disinfect needles ... hot water?"

"Yes, it does," he insisted, preparing his emaciated left arm for his repayment.

"That's how come I don't have the AIDS."

CHAPTER 30

Falling

I had to get out!

I raced to the kitchen, yanked open the utensils drawer and grabbed the chef's knife, then ran back to the passage. I hacked away at the lock, hacked away at the door, leaving deep gouges in the wood, stripping the white paint.

I had to get into that cupboard.

She had locked the phone in there and I needed it to call Adbul. I had money this time, for fuck's sake, and I wouldn't even be lying.

I had R300. Three hundred fucking rand.

I stole it from the purse in her handbag locked in a cupboard in her bedroom. She slept with the key to that cupboard under her pillow, inside the pillowcase, so I waited hours for her to fall into a deep sleep before slipping into her room and lying down gently on the bed next to her, then manoeuvring my hand inside the pillowcase and removing the key. I unlocked the cupboard and retrieved the money from the purse, then did everything in reverse. All with the stealth of a ninja. Then I waited patiently for sunrise, waited for the sounds of her stirring and the familiar sounds of her getting ready for work. It was all going according to schedule until she stopped in at the doorway of my room.

"Where's the money?" she asked.

I feigned sleepiness and then ignorance. "What money?"

"There's R300 missing from my wallet. I don't know how … I want it back." Her arms were folded across her chest and she was shaking slightly.

I sat up, pulling the duvet up to my chest. "I don't have it."

She turned and walked away and I lay down, listening to her unplugging the phone, then walking across to the passage cupboard and locking it inside. She left the flat, locking me in as usual, wordlessly. That's when I jumped up and frantically attacked the door of the passage cupboard.

I had to get out.

I ran around the flat opening and closing all the cupboard doors that weren't locked looking for God-knows-what. I got to the linen cupboard and paused. I ran my hand up and down the cotton sheets slowly, thoughtfully. I went back to my room and pulled on a pair of jeans, a vest and sneakers and packed my old school pencil case with my needles and teaspoon and lighters and the money into my small backpack.

I was going to get out.

I returned to the linen cupboard and pulled out four double-bed sheets and marched through to the lounge. I pushed aside the net curtains and opened the window on the left. I looked down. Two storeys down. Four sheets would be enough. I set to work tying the corners of the sheets to each other. I felt like I was fucking MacGyver. When I had finished tying the knots, I stood up, went over to the window and pushed it as far out as it would go, then tied one end of the makeshift sheet rope to the window restrictor, double-knotting it and tugging to make sure it was secure. I then threw my sheet rope out of the window and watched as it flapped, then came to rest against the side of the building. I slid my backpack onto my back, grabbed the window frame with one hand and hoisted myself up onto the ledge. I turned around slowly, then released my grip from the frame and grabbed the sheets with both hands and started lowering myself out of the window.

I was out.

What I hadn't counted on was my ineffectual knot-tying skills combined with my own body weight. I was less than a metre down the side of the building when the knot tying the first to the second sheet unravelled suddenly and swiftly. I went plummeting two storeys to the ground below, landed on the grass, breaking the fall with my lower back, my head striking the ground with a loud *thwack!*

My body went limp and cold. Was I paralysed?

Move. Move. Just Fucking Move.

I willed myself to move any body part. Slowly I rolled my head to the right, just in time to see the building supervisor watering the flowerbeds, his eyes wide.

"Good morning," I said, cheerily.

He raised his hand and proceeded to water the brick paving.

Get up. Get up. Get Fucking Up.

Feeling was returning to my body in the form of pins and needles. I sat up slowly, then stood up. Nothing broken. I bundled up the tangled mess of sheets, took the lift up to the flat and shoved them in through the security gates, then took the lift down again. As I exited the main gate in the direction of the taxi rank, I looked back and saw the one sheet still hanging out of the window like some gigantic flag of surrender.

I had gotten out.

CHAPTER 31

Always Bring a Banner to an Intervention

"I want to introduce you to a very powerful man," he said, jerkily shifting the gears of the old Corolla.

"Sure."

I was high. He was five years sober. We were driving along the winding coastal road to Scarborough, the expansive turquoise sea stretching out towards the endless horizon, the sun reflecting silver and dazzling off the gently rolling waves. I had an intellectual understanding that it was a beautiful view but, man, I was so fucking wasted.

I had met Jonathan a few weeks before outside the church hall in Woodstock where they held the Narcotics Anonymous meeting. I'd gotten a lift there with another guy, Cedric, but he had palmed me off on Jonathan during the coffee break. I overheard him saying, "Please take this chick home. She's fucking mad." Jonathan had obliged – that night and almost every night that followed, even coming upstairs to my mother's flat in Wynberg to meet her. I think she was relieved and comforted by the fact that he was a tall, older English man with pale blue eyes and high cheekbones and blond-grey hair. That is to say, I think she was relieved he was white. Subversive racist that she was. Jonathan dutifully dragged my loaded ass to meetings on a daily basis, entirely without any investment on my part. He just kept pitching up at the flat and driving me to wherever they were "carrying the message" that night. Unrelenting and somewhat annoying, he was interfering with my using in a big way.

"Do you want to get clean?" he had asked one evening on the ride home.

"Yes, I've been trying for almost a year." That was a lie. "I just don't know how." That was the truth.

So here we were, traipsing across the Deep South to meet someone who could apparently help me – when I secretly knew I was way beyond help. I think he knew that, too, which is why he was calling in this secret superpower. We drove down the one tiny main road in Scarborough and took a few turns before pulling into the driveway of a small ramshackle double-storey A-frame wooden cottage. It was not where I envisioned a "powerful man" living. I had imagined a sprawling mansion. I associated power with money. With drugs. The short, bespectacled coloured man making his way down the driveway to meet us did not look as though he had either of those: money or drugs.

I climbed out of the car and went to stand next to Jonathan who was already greeting the man with a warm hug. These huggers. What the fuck was up with all the touchy-feely hugging?

"This is Fonnie," said Jonathan. I half-smiled and partially raised my hand in greeting. "This is the girl I was telling you about."

I scowled at Jonathan. I was used to being talked about – by my family mostly – but I didn't like the idea that this man knew more about me than I did about him. I hated that disadvantage. From what I could see, I wasn't sure he could be of any help to me. He was only about a head and a half taller than me, greying hair, severely nicotine-stained teeth and he spoke with a thick coloured – and I surmised – largely uneducated accent.

He led us inside, into the dark, cluttered lounge, and gestured for me to sit on the green corduroy-upholstered armchair.

"So, tell me," he drew a cigarette from a packet of Winston and lit it, "what have you tried to do to get sober?"

"NA." I nodded at Jonathan. "I went to a shitty rehab in Piketberg a few months ago but that didn't work. It had goats. I've tried detoxing on my own, but it never works." My voice was tinged with defensiveness and arrogance.

He took another drag. "And you want recovery?"

I paused. What if I said, no? Why were these people always asking this fucking question?

"Yes. I have nothing left."

Fonnie and Jonathan exchanged knowing glances and I scratched my right arm. I was starting to withdraw. Fucksake. And I was on the other side of the bloody world!

"Jonathan and I want to talk for a while," said Fonnie. It was more of a statement than a request. "My daughter is outside. You can talk to her."

I pushed myself up out of the armchair and headed out the front door. I found the sunset on the other side. Golden, pink-purple skies. Hypothetically beautiful. I also found the daughter. A petite, pretty young thing who could not have been older than 11.

"I'm Tracey-Lee." She offered me her hand and I took it. She led me down a path to a set of wooden swings and we sat swinging together, side by side, sometimes in silence and sometimes talking about absolutely normal things.

It was the most surreal experience I had had in a long time.

The junkie and the innocent child, swinging on the swings, talking about boys, crushes and how much we hated school.

"What does your dad do?" I asked, pushing my feet down against the gravel to make the swing go higher.

"He helps people," came her reply. I bit my lip. Not this person.

As though reading my mind, she stated confidently, "Don't worry. He will definitely help you too."

CHAPTER 32

All the Best People are Mad

Fonnie's suggestion had been that I attend the Cape Town Drug Counselling Centre's outpatient programme while I waited for a bed at an inpatient facility. I was high every time I attended the sessions at the centre. They knew it and I knew it. I didn't realise at the time that they thought I was insane, but that's how I found myself walking up the tarred hill to the Groote Schuur Hospital, three quarters of heroin, tightly wrapped in plastic, nestled deeply in my damp fist. As I laboured up the hill, I tried to figure out how I was going to smuggle it into the psychiatric ward. So, as I crossed the busy intersection, I decided to use before I went in. I approached a sleepy-looking security guard and asked him for directions to Ward C23. Reluctantly, he stood up from his broken swivel chair, tore his attention away from the small, fuzzy black-and-white television screen and exited the cramped booth.

"Up the road, second building on your left. Psychiatry. They will tell you from there." He disappeared back into his wooden hut.

I located the Psychiatry building and found another security guard on duty at a long L-shaped desk.

"Can I use your bathroom please?"

He pointed down the hall. In the toilets I cooked and shot up a whole quarter. I leaned back against the cool cistern. I still had the problem of the other two quarters, as well as the needle and spoon. There was no way I could bring my works into the ward. I pulled at the end of the roll of toilet paper, unwound several sheets and wrapped them around the charred spoon and syringe. I dropped it in the sanitary towel bin and immediately felt immense sadness. I would need to snort what I smuggled in. I must have been in the toilet too long for the security guard's liking, and there was a sudden insistent knock on the door.

"Lady! Are you okay?"

"I'm fine ..." I added as much sobriety to my voice as I could muster. "I'll be out now."

I shoved first one quarter then another into my mouth, as far back as they could go, until they had settled snugly behind my molars. I grabbed my backpack and exited. The guard was standing right outside, much taller than he had seemed seated behind the desk.

"*Waar wil jy wees*?" he asked gruffly.

"C23," I said, testing out my vocals skills with my new dental modifications. His menacing look suddenly changed to one of understanding, almost empathy. Ah, another *malletjie*, he must have thought. He escorted me down a long passageway, then another, until we stopped at a glass door reinforced with diamond-shaped metal burglar bars. He pressed a bell mounted onto the wall. A few seconds later, the door was opened by a middle-aged, soft-eyed nurse wearing a starched white uniform with maroon epaulettes.

"This one is yours," announced the security guard and turned to leave. The nurse placed her hand under my elbow and led me inside, closing the door behind her with a decisive click.

"*Meisie*," she asked, "what's your name?"

"Desiree-Anne Martin." The contraband in my mouth was creating a lot of saliva. I sucked it back and swallowed hard.

"I'm Nurse Tessa," she said, letting go of my elbow and checking a list on the desk at the entrance. "Ah, there you are," she tapped a pen on the clipboard. "Cape Town Drug Counselling Centre. You're here for heroin detox." She clucked her tongue sympathetically. "You're in bed seven. I'll take you there and then we'll do all the paperwork once you're settled."

And that's exactly what she – what we – did.

"This is the men's section," she said, pointing to two lines of beds, most of them occupied, running from the wall to heavily barred windows. "This is the bathroom." She stopped and opened a door to reveal a toilet and a shower. There was no lock on the door. "And this is the women's section." It looked identical to the men's: two rows of about 10 hospital beds running the length of the room. There were about three or four entirely motionless bodies and a woman sitting on the edge of the farthest bed, rocking gently. I followed Nurse Tessa to the third bed from the end, which she indicated was mine and dropped my backpack on the bed.

She patted me on the shoulder.

"I'm going to have to search you and your belongings now."

"For what?" I asked, innocently, almost sounding affronted.

"For any dangerous weapons, sharp objects, anything you can hurt yourself with and drugs," she stated.

I sat down on the bed and started unzipping my bag. "Sure." I hadn't packed much. I didn't have much. She sat next to me, the bag between us, and thoroughly searched pockets and seams, turning clothes inside out. She emptied out my toiletry bag and confiscated my nail clippers – which I used to snip open quarters; like my hair, my nails hadn't grown in years. She placed them in a plastic Ziploc bag, which she produced from her pocket.

"You can pack all of this in there," she said, pointing to the small cupboard next to the bed. She stood up and signalled for me to do the same. "And now for you."

I probed the quarters at the back of my mouth with the tip of my tongue to make sure they were still there and push them down as far as they could go. Nurse Tessa patted me down from head to toe, made me turn my pockets inside out, made me loosen and shake out my hair and remove and shake out my shoes. She asked me to lift my T-shirt and expertly slid her hand under the band of my bra and swept her hand all the way around.

"Looks like we're all good. I'll come back and fill in the paperwork with you soon."

I stood frozen. Had I really just gotten away with that?

"Oh, wait," she laughed as though remembering something funny, and turned back. "Can you just open your mouth for me really wide please?"

Fuck.

I obeyed and she peered inside my mouth, which felt wet and gobby. She placed her spectacles, which hung around her neck on a neon-yellow string, on her eyes and looked around.

Please, dear God. My random prayer went up to the heavens.

She removed her spectacles. "You have such lovely teeth. Why do you use heroin?"

She shook her head and clucked her tongue again as she walked away and I sank down onto the bed and immediately broke into a sweat.

They caught me.

I had been trying to snort lines in the toilet. I'd torn a page out of *The Lord of The Rings*, a book I had borrowed from one of the male patients who I befriended within hours of arriving. I had torn it into an even smaller piece and had rolled it up and carried it, hidden in the palm of my hand, into the bathroom. It was a bit flimsy, but it would have to do. I'd removed one of the quarters and bitten off the end then, as I had nothing to cut the lines with, slowly tapped two fat lines on the toilet seat. There was no cover and there was no cistern block. I had just finished schnarfing the second line when the door swung open and there was a nurse. I stood back against the wall while she dusted the rest of the powder into the toilet bowl and removed the rest of the quarter and the rolled-up paper from my hand. She was still berating me in Afrikaans as she lead me back to my bed.

It was only when I got there that I realised I had accidentally swallowed the other quarter.

It never occurred to me not to. It never occurred to me that this was the ultimate act of insanity and desperation. It never occurred to me that it very definitely classified me as a bona fide addict. It never occurred to me that, by this very act alone, I had a serious problem. For the next three days, every time I defecated, I would do so into toilet paper held in my hand under my ass. Then I would search through my own faeces, looking for that quarter of heroin.

CHAPTER 33

Ethnic Violence

I had been hanging around the taxi rank for hours. Earlier that morning I had been discharged from C23 and walked straight down from the hospital to Mowbray to go score. I had been in the ward for five days and was deemed "medically detoxed" so I was looking forward to the smack hitting my pure, clean blood.

I wasn't the only one waiting. A few other junkies were loitering listlessly around the public telephones, trying every few minutes to phone their connect and cursing when it went straight to voicemail and the phone swallowed their precious coins.

There must be a shortage. Fuck, fuck, fuck.

Liam, a fellow junkie and former schoolmate, galloped down the slopes from the train station and, half-winded, hair wet with sweat, asked, "Where's Sam?"

"Don't know. There's no one here."

"Fuck!" he exclaimed, as he began gnawing at the plastic hospital identity band around his wrist.

"You come from hospital?" I asked.

"Yeah, I just ran away. OD-ed last night." He spat the bits of plastic and paper out onto the pavement. "But I need a fucking fix."

"I wish I could help."

"Sure," he said, distracted, scanning the taxi rank. "I'll go look for Adbul." And he trotted off in the direction of the dealer's

Durban Road flat. I knew Adbul wasn't home; I'd stopped off there half an hour earlier and there had been no answer to my incessant, agitated banging on his door.

I sat down on the pavement outside the public toilets, trying in vain to block out the pervasive stench of urine, and stretched out my legs. I didn't care that I was in a jade-green vintage crocheted dress and heeled sandals. I always tried to take pride in my appearance lest someone discover my secret – and also to attract clients. But when the turkey hits, you just don't care.

The taxis swerved into the rank, avoiding the potholes at the entrance. The heavy, toxic smell of petrol permeated the place and the sound of *gaatjies* yelling distant destinations rose above the rattling of the trains as they passed nearby. The taxi rank was marked out with invisible lines. Near the toilets was the Congo, near the subway entrance was Tanzania and on the far side, at the phones, was Nigeria.

"Who you wait for?" A heavy accented voice.

I looked up and, shielding my eyes from the sun with my hand, made out the silhouette of a stranger. I took the opportunity.

"You, of course."

Prostitution had become a necessary evil, like Astroturf. He reached out his hand and pulled me up from the pavement.

"Come."

"Where are we going?"

"To the house. Come."

I surreptitiously disengaged my hand from his, but followed close on his heels across the taxi rank, struggling with the small, steep incline at the perimeter. Stupid heels. He helped me down the other side and we crossed the road. A car drove past and I avoided the driver's pejorative stare. We walked up a short driveway, rubbish littering what used to be a lawn and flowerbed: discarded quartz beer bottles, torn plastic bags and a teat from a baby bottle.

The house was old, in the style of that suburb.

Lurid green paint peeled off the walls and some of the window frames held flattened cardboard boxes instead of glass. The front door was bright red. Inside there was no furniture other than a soiled mattress in the corner of the front room. Two of the interleading doors were shut, but I could see into the kitchen. Two men sat on upturned crates, smoking. They looked at me, hungrily. Words were exchanged in a language I did not understand. One of them laughed a bit too jovially.

"So we have sex, yes?" He beat his fist against his chest.

I had to think quickly. I looked at the front door.

"No," I feigned a girlish giggle, "I can't. I have my period."

"Eh?"

"Bleeding," I pointed at my nether regions. "I'm bleeding."

He inched slowly towards me as the other two got up from their crates, framing the doorway.

"Sex, now."

"I can't. I said I'm …"

"Then why you come here?"

The fear singed my eyes. I felt like what I was, a helpless victim to the circling vultures.

Don't cry. Don't fucking cry.

I backed away and was almost up against the front door when a loud, decisive knock made me lurch forward. He shoved me aside and opened the door a fraction. More exchanges in a foreign tongue. He opened it wider and there stood Sam, my other dealer.

With a robotic gesture of his hand, he let me pass.

Sam grabbed me by the wrist and near-dragged me back down the driveway. He considered me his 'girlfriend'; I fucked him for money and drugs too, but he was unaware of my arrangement with Adbul, who was one of his runners. He cared for me, I thought. He bought me food, which was entirely wasted on me. He even bought me a Lotto ticket once and that made me feel what may have been affection towards him. He wanted me to stop using even though he sold and gave me heroin almost daily. He wanted to clean me up so I could be his proper girlfriend. He had even taken me to see the "Junkie Shrink" so I could get a script for Subutex and Dormicum to aid me through withdrawal. He paid for the medication and I used it all while still injecting smack. Sam was sweet and protective and utterly deluded. I fell into the girlfriend role as easily as any other persona I adopted and extorted as much of anything that I could from him.

Now he was dragging me across the road, back towards the taxi rank.

"Those are Nigerians. They will carve you up. Don't ever go there again. Don't ever make me go there again."

"I'm sorry, baby," I said, with not a tinge of remorse in my voice. "Do you have any smack for me please?"

CHAPTER 34

Testing Negative

I regained consciousness with my face half-submerged in water. I was in the bath and the water was freezing. My blurred mother was hovering over the bath.

"Are you okay, are you okay?" she kept repeating, breathlessly.

The last thing I remembered was having taken a yoghurt out of the fridge and then ... nothing.

I had overdosed.

I sat up in the bath and realised I was still fully dressed. I realised, too, that my 64-year-old mother had carried me from the kitchen to the bathroom and deposited me in the tub of cold water.

New Year's Day. I'd been prowling the flat like a caged animal in the pitch dark the night before, not allowed out, not allowed anywhere, literally pacing up and down, wanting, needing, craving. When morning came, I had managed to phone Abdul from the house phone and got him to deliver two quarters directly to the flat: he had thrown it in through the bathroom window and I had tossed the money out. It had all been executed with military precision. I was elated. I shot up inside my cupboard because I was no longer allowed to use the toilet and close the door – I had to leave the door open – and then went to grab a tub of yoghurt from the fridge. That's when I lost consciousness.

Now, I could hear my mother on the phone to Jonathan. Fuck. Why was she involving him?

"She says she isn't using and I don't know how she would have gotten it …" she was whispering. "Okay … Yes, I'm sorry … Are you sure? … Okay … See you now."

My mother came to sit at the end of my bed.

"Your lips were turning blue. You're telling me you aren't on drugs?"

I tied back my hair, "Mom, where would I get drugs from? Seriously?"

"Jonathan's coming now. He's taking you to Victoria Hospital for a drug test."

I widened my eyes, feigning innocence.

"Why do I need a drug test? I just got dizzy and passed out. That's all."

She stood up. "You're going. That's final."

Jonathan arrived, with a young Jewish boy, David, in tow. Both were appropriately disenchanted that they were dragging some junkie to test for the obvious on News Year's Day.

"We were in the middle of David's Step 5, you know?" grumbled Jonathan, buckling his seat belt. David, short, with curly hair, turned his brown eyes on me and gave me a most disapproving look. I didn't give a fuck. We drove to the hospital in silence. Jonathan parked the car and as we got out he turned to me and said, "You may as well just admit you used."

"But I didn't!" I retorted. At Enquiries, Jonathan informed the thin, weary-looking nurse that we needed a drug test done. She jerked her head in the direction of a room to the left.

"Over there," she said. "Go inside, fill this in and take a seat."

Jonathan and I parted company and I followed her directions to the nurses' station. I stepped inside the small cubicle, sat down and filled in my fake details. Then I waited and waited. Eventually another plump, overworked nurse joined me in the cubicle.

"I'm Sister Johannes. What test are we doing?"

I didn't hesitate. "Pregnancy test."

She rummaged through the cupboard, then presented me with

a plastic container.

"Toilet is in there. Pee in the cup and bring it back to me."

I obeyed her instructions, filling the cup with urine and returning it to her within minutes. She tore open the packet housing the pregnancy test and dipped the stick into the urine sample for a few seconds.

We waited.

"It's negative."

I feigned relief. "Thank goodness! Sister, do you mind telling my friend the result please?"

She frowned but agreed and we exited the cubicle.

Jonathan stood up from the bench where he and David had been sitting. Sister Johannes, without a trace of emotion in her voice, announced, "The test result is negative," turned and shuffled down the passageway. Jonathan looked utterly dumbfounded.

"See," I said, "I told you I was clean."

I felt smug and silently congratulated myself on my cleverness and quick thinking. But my elation waned as Jonathan drove me back to the flat. I knew I couldn't continue this life-that-wasn't-a-life any more, trying to fool everyone when the only person I was kidding was myself. As much as I hated them, attending NA meetings had inadvertently taught me that.

Sanctimonious, self-righteous fuckers. I had overdosed four or five times by now, furious that none of them had ended in actual death. I was so exhausted. I wanted to use. I wanted to die. I wanted to use until I died.

The only other option was this recovery thing, but they wouldn't let me use drugs. I felt like a zombie. The doctor my mother had taken me to had warned that I'd be dead in two months if I carried on. Two months wasn't that long to wait.

CHAPTER 35

Taking Care of Business

Two weeks later, I was arrested. I found myself tucked between two women like the filling in a criminal sandwich. One woman had buried her face into the back of my neck. I tried not to stiffen as I felt her warm, moist breath on my skin, stale and sweet like a mixture of cheap cigarettes and cherry-flavoured lollipops. She had curled her left arm around my waist, her hand tucked under my hipbone. She pulled me closer as she stirred in her sleep, murmuring softly.

How could she sleep? Perhaps she was used to this, sleeping in jail.

We lay on the thin, blue vinyl mattresses like those padded ones used in gym classes, only these were mouldy and curled up at the corners. The older woman had warned against using the coarse, grey blankets because of the possibility of catching lice and other vermin or germs. Fuck. I had used the blanket the night before when I had been alone. The cold cement had singed my skin and I had needed to keep warm. I was wearing what I was arrested in: a pair of oversized jeans and a thin, strappy vest. And trainers devoid of their laces. I was bone-cold. I was exhausted. I needed to sleep but couldn't.

I kept my eyes closed and tried to remember what night it was. Sunday? Yes, Sunday. I had been there since Friday, which was a wholly amateur mistake of the highest order because everyone knew that you just don't get arrested on a Friday because then you'll sit for three days. But I had overdosed in the public toilets at St Peter's Square in Observatory. The shopping centre was built on an old graveyard and as diggers were violently excavating and removing the decomposed flesh, brittle bones and crumbling headstones in the final resting place of the once-beloved, I remember thinking that something really bad was going to happen there. It hadn't occurred to me that, years later, the bad thing would happen to me.

In the centre's clean toilet cubicle, I remembered tapping the heroin into the charred teaspoon and knowing – *just knowing* – that it was too much, but I cooked it and shot up anyway. I hadn't wanted to go back out because then I'd have had to have sex with Abdul who had given me the drugs.

I came to, sprawled out on the floor of the toilet stall. A grim, pimply-faced paramedic had hovered over me and explained how the cleaning woman had called him to kick the door down when she heard me crash against the metal door and onto the floor. I had lain motionless, unconscious and she had freaked out. I stumbled up from the floor and tried to manoeuvre past him but he blocked the doorway.

"You have to wait for the police."

"I'm fine, it's really fine …" I tried to bargain. But he stood firm, blocking my only escape.

The police came eventually, though the heroin made the details very blurry. There was a blood test and fingerprints were taken, but how I got to the various places remained cloaked in opioid-drenched mystery.

I had been alone in the holding cell Friday night too, withdrawing badly. I imagined there had been a raging rainstorm and that the building had a tin roof with loose sheeting that banged incessantly in the howling wind. Or perhaps I had hallucinated – it was mid-January and the height of summer? Had someone come to see me? A lawyer, yes. He appeared on the other side of the bars in the middle of the night, looking all dodgy and desperate.

"You don't belong in here," he'd said.

I agreed, of course, but thought, "Dude, you don't really know me."

That was two long nights ago. I stretched my aching legs and my stomach grumbled, protesting the self-inflicted three-day starvation. I couldn't even imagine eating the boiled eggs tinged purple from overcooking or the stale bread that was brought to the cell door three times a day. I had tried a bite of the bread the day before, but the dry chunk had lodged in my throat and I had vomited almost immediately into the grimy, stainless steel toilet in the corner of the cell. I hadn't used the toilet for any other purpose other than to vomit. I had willed my bladder and bowels to cease functioning for the weekend; not a hard thing to do if you're a heroin junkie.

By the muted light entering the barred opening high up in the wall, I knew it was nearly Monday morning. Thank God. Glory, a young and hyperactive (or high) girl, had told me that we would be taken to Caledon Square the next morning to appear in court. "Someone must come bail you out. Otherwise," she warned, "it's Pollsmoor for you."

Glory had come in Sunday morning along with a few other women. All prostitutes, all in various states of undress. All protesting their innocence and all colourfully cursing the unborn children of the police officers who dragged them in. Glory – whose real name was Annemarie and who was raised on a farm a million memories away – said that it happened every weekend, but that this weekend was especially bad because there were 14 of us in the small cell. She took a liking to me, said she liked my posh way of speaking and my hair.

She asked if I was a whore and I said, "Yes. Just a different kind of one."

She said, "All women are whores so don't worry, *skattie*." She disapproved of my heroin use and said that *kak* would kill me. Her slender brown wrists housed vicious, raised scars. I could not stop staring.

"Oh these? One night I went to see a man who lived in a fancy house by the beach. He drugged me and put hooks in my wrists and tied me up so I was hanging from the ceiling by my wrists. My ankles, too, so I was like a star. He went out for a *bietjie* so I pulled myself out of them, pulled the hooks through my flesh and ran away. Later, I found out that the crazy fucking bastard killed two other girls."

"And then?" I asked, transfixed.

"Then?" she looked puzzled. "Then nothing. I bandaged them up and they got better. What else can you do?"

It was Glory who announced the arrival of the morning, along with the now-familiar jangling of heavy metal keys in the adjacent cells.

"Everybody up! Time to do the washing!" she shouted.

I sat up and looked around. Every last woman was removing her pants or skirt followed by her panties. Seeing the confusion on my face, Meisie – another sweet whore who had confided in me that she was only working the streets to support her three-year-old child ("So I'll just do it for two more years, you see?") – leaned down and offered an explanation.

"You can't have a dirty stink panty. You need to wash your panty and your pussy. It has to be clean. Your pussy is your purse, girl."

I was directed to wash my panties under the tap in the silver basin and hang it up alongside the others on the bars of the cell door. A variety of multicoloured, patterned underwear hung in rows, like flags proudly claiming territory. It was like a big 'fuck you' to the wardens. Pure brilliance. A few hours later, we were squashed – in our damp underwear – into the back of a police van and on our way to The Gat.

I hoped to all hell someone would be on the other end to bail me out.

It was my dad who had come to post bail, an hour before the police van was set to take all offenders whose families didn't give a fuck or those who no longer had anyone to call any more to Pollsmoor Correctional Facility. I was relieved to see him standing in the court. I had no one left other than my mom and dad. I had pushed all my friends away in favour of the needle. I really missed my best friend Diana; my addiction had utterly destroyed that relationship. The last time I had seen her, she had invited me to her house for home-cooked supper but I was so smacked up that I kept feeding the food to the dog under the table. I later realised she didn't even have a dog.

After standing in the dock and pleading Not Guilty to the charge of possession on the advice of my Uncle Sydney, who was my lawyer now, I was released and the case was postponed until August. It was only January. I had plenty of time to sort out my shit or die before then. My dad was grim-faced when I met him in the cavernous hallway outside the court.

"Your Uncle Edward died on Friday. He had a heart attack."

I already knew this because my only visitor to the holding cells, Jonathan from NA, had broken the news. I felt nothing except anger that my uncle's death had overshadowed my arrest and had probably been the reason why my mother had left me in the cells the whole weekend.

"And we found the gold-plated cutlery you stole from your mother," he added.

I knew they would have found the six shiny 24-carat plated golden teaspoons in my bag at Woodstock police station and given them and the rest of my belongings to someone. I had intended to pawn them but overdosing had interrupted those plans.

My father took me back to his place, stopping at the pharmacy on the way to buy lice shampoo. His girlfriend and I smoked tik in the bathroom at his flat while I brushed the shampoo through my thick, knotted hair with a fine comb.

"I'm taking you back to your mother. You can't stay here," my dad announced when we emerged from the bathroom an hour later. I didn't really want to stay with him and his oversized, under-aged tik whore girlfriend. I knew going back to my mom would be inevitable, but I really didn't want to face her either; not after the arrest, after my uncle's death and having heard that she had been given two month's notice by her landlord that same weekend. She would be in a righteously pissy mood, all things considered. And she would resort to locking me up in the flat again like a prisoner. I couldn't tolerate that idea, not again. I would need to get out somehow or find a way to get Abdul to deliver, with my usual empty promises of money or real promises of sex.

I would have to make a plan. Or die – again – trying.

PART 4

The New Rules

CHAPTER 36

Powerlessness and Damages

"You sure this is what you want?" my mother asked, waving the rehab admission cheque in my face. "You have your court case coming up in two months' time, in August. You absolutely sure you want to go?"

I had just stolen R1800 worth of smack from Abdul two days before so, yes, I was more than a bit keen to get the fuck out of Dodge. I really, *really* needed to get away. What I wanted more than anything was a small break from using and to get away from Abdul for a while and to learn how to use successfully and go back home. Maybe use every second day or only on weekends.

Now, it had been three days and, so far, no one was teaching me any of that shit. Instead there were Powerlessness and Damages Groups and Feelings Groups and Step Work and Narcotics Anonymous meetings and even fucking prayers.

I dug my thumbnails deeper into the woollen fabric of the jersey, trying to make holes at the cuffs for my thumbs to go through. I had nearly broken through; then I could tuck my hands into the sleeves so that they weren't so fucking cold all the time. I called it my 'turkey jersey'. Warm enough to stave off the bone-chilling cold but not too warm that I sweated like a pig at the slightest shift in temperature. My hands were always freezing though, so I needed to make these makeshift thumb loops. It was a good task to while away the time during yet another Powerlessness and Damages Group session.

Lisa was talking. She was always talking, jabbering away incessantly about arbitrary rubbish. Mainly about herself, about the lavish lifestyle provided for her by her sugar daddy, about how being here was a waste of her time and his money. All of her clothes were expensive and she was a self-proclaimed "label whore". Her shiny blonde curls bounced when she spoke – which was *all the time*. She reminded me of one of those dogs at the back of cars with the heads that bob up and down. Her accent exposed her as an unfortunate white-trash casualty. I think she fabricated half the shit. Hell, I made up half the shit myself but at least mine sounded plausible. My dad had taught me that: if you're going to lie, keep it as close to the truth as possible. He also told me to never mix my drinks. I listened to my daddy.

"You started telling us about your relationship yesterday," Anton, the senior counsellor, turned to me. He uncrossed and then crossed his impossibly long legs. "Why don't you tell us more?"

I slid down in my curved plastic chair and planted my feet on the ground, knees apart. I was almost parallel to the floor.

"There's nothing more to tell," I said, focusing my attention on my right thumbnail. "We met, he told me he was a junkie, I tried to get him clean – that was a fucking joke – then I gave up and here I am." I ended with a flourish of my hands and an unspoken *ta-dah!* Anton's face – dotted with old acne scars and deeply embedded blackheads – was, as always, passive.

"Tell us about how you met. Explain that part to the group."

I looked around.

Sydney, Aslam, Lisa, Dale, Ryan, Stacey.

Juicer, Tik-kop, Crackhead, Tik-kop, Cokehead, Tik-kop.

I really did not want to share the most personal and intimate details of my life with these random addicts in this tiny, airless room.

"So, tell the group about that part of your relationship," his tone was still calm but more insistent. I shifted up in my chair – though my feet could barely reach the floor – and crossed my legs, tucking my left foot behind my right ankle. I had realised I could do that the day before, which meant my legs were extremely thin. Gap-between-the-thighs skinny. I'd also noticed that my clothes were ill fitting and too big for me. I was practically drowning in 'turkey jersey'. I hadn't had the balls to look at myself in the mirror yet.

"Well," I said, "at first he wanted nothing to do with me and I pursued him heavily, almost obsessively. Wherever he went, I somehow turned up. I was convinced we were meant to be together. I was convinced he was The One."

"So you stalked him?" asked Sydney, matter-of-factly. I ignored him. I couldn't expect these people to understand, least of all a geriatric alcoholic.

"Then one night we were out, he was a complete dick to me and shoved me out of his car the next morning and told me to fuck off."

"You wanted to be in a relationship with this asshole?" exclaimed Dale. Dale had tried to corner and kiss me in the kitchen pantry over a box of sugared cornflakes that morning, so his motives for asking the question were sketchy.

I looked him straight in his big brown eyes. "Yes, I did. I was in love with him." Dale snorted derisively. I rolled my eyes at him, but returned to chewing nervously on my left thumbnail.

"Carry on," urged Anton.

I inspected my nail. The cuticle was almost entirely bitten off now.

"So I wrote a five-page letter to the universe."

Laughter erupted.

"To who now?" asked Stacey. Her voice was barely above a whisper. It was rarely louder.

I cringed slightly. "To God basically."

"I don't believe in God," announced Lisa, grabbing the gap. "I think—"

Anton intervened. "This isn't about your beliefs, Lisa. It's about Desiree's and we should respect them. The preamble says 'no judgement'. Lets allow her to finish." Lisa pursed her lips and looked appropriately injured.

I slumped back down in the chair.

"I wrote a long letter; I bargained with God. I told him what I wanted and said what I would do in exchange. It had all sorts of things in it, about how I would take better care of myself and be a better person ... One of the things I asked for was The Big Love, The One and—"

"What else did you ask for? I would have *lekker* asked for drugs!" exclaimed Aslam. More collective laughter. Anton hushed the group back into silence.

"It doesn't matter," I sighed. "The point is that a few minutes later my doorbell rang and it was him. He wanted to come in and I hesitated at first but then let him in. You know how one decision can change the course of your life? Well ..." I trailed off.

"And then?" asked Anton.

"He apologised, gave me drugs and later told me he wanted me to be his girlfriend. Then he told me he was a heroin addict."

"Whoa ..." whispered Stacey. "What did you do?"

"I had no idea what to say, but I dove in. I was sure I could change him with all the love I had to give."

"Wait a minute," said Ryan. He had just arrived that morning. Blond hair and green-blue eyes. Yummy, fresh meat. "What's your drug of choice again?"

"Heroin."

CHAPTER 37

Fraternising is Another Word for Fucking

"Who has 10 sugars in their coffee?"

We were at the coffee station in the lounge, preparing our legal morning fix.

"Who has three coffees in their coffee?" Ryan retorted, slowly stirring his pale brown, sad, sugary liquid.

"Coffee is all I have left," I sighed. "That and beautiful, lovely cigarettes."

"And sex. You could have sex." His tone was part accurate, part suggestive.

"No. No, I couldn't," I said firmly.

"You don't have sex?" He had managed to skilfully scan the entire length of my person before asking.

"I don't have sex in rehab," I shook my head, adding milk to my steaming mug. "Last time I did, I thought the guy had brought smack back in with him. They found us and I got called a whore, a slut, and got kicked out."

"Jesus! What rehab was that?"

"You wouldn't know it. It was way out in the sticks and it had no programme, and staff were using and it had goats." He laughed.

"No, I'm serious." I continued, "I hate goats." I shivered and tried to dislodge the memory, pack it away. "I remember walking in there and 'Hotel California' was playing on the radio in the skanky kitchen. You know that song?"

"Kinda."

"Well, there's a line 'You can check out any time you like but you can never leave.' That was basically a sign of things to come. I didn't have medical aid so I couldn't go to any of the classy rehabs, so I ended up with a group of serious junkies and criminals and liars and thieves. I was completely freaked out. The owner was a 'recovered' crack addict whose story was that he walked into a park one night a total crackhead and saw the Light or some shit and walked out sober and stayed that way. He was dodgy as fuck and hardly around, off using probably, so he left these untrained, barely sober – some even using – 'counsellors' in charge. One of those so-called counsellors was a friend of Darren's. He was insanely violent and the junkiest junkie I knew. It was out of control. It was a total joke." My coffee was getting cold but I felt almost obligated to tell this story. Rehab was having a weird effect on me.

Fucksake.

"There was an energy healer there – I forget her name," I continued, sipping then adding more boiled water to my cup. "She said she'd been sent there to help heal the addicts. I liked her but she was swimming upstream without a paddle. She said I should take out all my piercings because my soul was leaking out of the holes I'd created. She was a bit cooked but she had good intentions. But for the rest of the time we sat around and did literally nothing and just smoked cigarettes, talked about how much drugs we used to use and plotted our escape, usually involving the freight trains that ran every few hours down by the tracks a few blocks down."

"Did you? Run away, I mean?" Ryan was sitting on the arm of the couch and I couldn't tell if he was genuinely interested in my tale of rehab riotousness. But I carried on anyway. If this was his idea of flirting, then he deserved to hear the whole, depressing story.

"I didn't, but some of the boys did – and then were inevitably dragged back a few days later by their parents. That's when I slept with the one kid – he was a teenager and I was 26 – because he had come back in and I thought he was carrying."

"So it didn't work?" he asked, earnestly.

"Getting drugs from him?"

"No, man, the rehab?" he laughed.

"I'm here, aren't I?" I couldn't curb my sarcasm. I sighed again, feeling an actual twinge of pain in my chest. "Then came the slut-shaming and they said I had to go. I left … and that was the beginning of the end."

We carried our now tepid mugs of coffee onto the veranda. This place, Akron House, was so different to Piketberg in every way. It was calm and containing and it was clean, a far cry from the previous smut hole. It felt safe too. And no fucking goats.

With my free hand I rummaged in my hoodie pocket for my cigarettes. I found the box, flipped open the top and drew a single cigarette out with my teeth, then wrapped my lips around the filter. Ryan leaned forward and offered me a light.

"They introduced me to Pink Floyd there. Made us watch *The Wall*. I heard the song 'Comfortably Numb' for the first time. It was a seminal moment. But that's all that place was good for."

"You use big words. It's very attractive."

I looked at him with a mixture of disdain and amusement.

"So that's a no to the sex then?" he asked, hopefully.

I inhaled deeply, then exhaled slowly. "Just drink your sugar, Ryan."

CHAPTER 38

Diamonds are Forever

"But you could've gotten caught," said Anton.

"Could've, but didn't."

I sat cross-legged on the chair. Anton's legs were stretched out, taking up the space between us in the small session room. There was a framed watercolour painting of a seascape that reminded me of Brighton beach.

"But you could be in jail right now."

"But I'm not." I linked my fingers and stretched them, cracking the knuckles of both hands. It was a nervous habit I had had since childhood.

"Where were the drugs?" he continued, ignoring my blatant passive-aggression.

"In my shoes. In the soles of my shoes. They hollowed out these Doc Marten-type shoes and packed them tight with heroin. And I wore those on the plane and into Mauritius."

"And Darren?"

"I wasn't *going* to carry," I ignored the question. "But I actually insisted. It was exciting. I wanted to be a drug smuggler."

"You give any thought to the consequences?"

"Not at all. I was scared and I knew I could get caught but I also didn't, if you know what I mean?"

Anton offered his usual slow, measured, sympathetic nod.

"We were supposed to be this couple on holiday. Lots of couples go on holiday to Mauritius, so it was a good cover."

"And where did he carry?" he asked again.

"I think he swallowed bullets of the stuff because I remember him practising at the house using fish oil and these fake bullets, condoms filled with sugar or something. But I honestly can't remember. It's all a bit blurry."

"What happened when you got there?"

"Darren disappeared for ages, took my shoes with him. I was in this crappy hotel room with an air conditioner that sounded like a chainsaw. It was so disgustingly humid. And I was turkey-ing and I couldn't tell him how bad it was because he didn't know how much I had been using, how much I had been stealing from his stash. But he came back with a crap ton of smack and we ended up having a really nice holiday. We hired scooters – which I crashed. We snorkelled – I nearly drowned. We went shopping – and shoplifting. So much fun." I sat bolt upright, unfolding my legs and dangling them over the edge of the chair. "We got engaged, you know? On the beach at sunset, church bells peeling in the background … amazing."

Anton's eyes instinctively went to my hands. I retracted them into my hoodie sleeves.

"It was beautiful. Diamond and amethyst." I felt an unfamiliar sensation in my chest. My head suddenly hurt. A tear trickled down my cheek and I wiped it away abruptly. "He pawned it … Sold the engagement ring for six quarters without telling me."

"All of this," he drew an imaginary circle in the air with his arms, "and you're still struggling to see your damages?"

I chewed the nail of my forefinger. These one-on-one sessions were a real pain in the ass. Why did he always have to be so … so … fucking right all the time?

I removed my finger from my mouth. "I guess."

"What do you guess?"

"I guess it wasn't the way I remember it." Another tear ran rebelliously down my other cheek.

"What are you feeling right now?" he asked, gently.

I didn't know. It just hurt. Every part of me, from my head to my heart, was on fire. My chest felt heavy like lead and my brain as though it might explode. Sadness? Anger? I hadn't felt a real feeling in years.

"I don't know."

"That's okay," he said, motioning to stand up. "We'll talk some more tomorrow. In Group."

Fan-Fucking-Tastic.

"Look," I said, earnestly, "I just don't like talking in Group."

He looked at me with a half-smile, a little condescending. "You're doing very well. I know you're a very private person, but you know what they say? 'Secrets keep you sick.'"

I groaned. "I hate those clichés!"

"They're clichés for a reason – because they're true. You have to start sharing if you want to get better."

"Can't I just tell you? In the one-on-ones?" I knew I was being manipulative and I knew he knew it too.

"We'll have our sessions, but I want you to share at least once in every group." He got up from the plastic chair, signalling the end of the 'emergency meeting' I had called. "Oh," he turned at the door, "and your life story is due on Tuesday."

I felt instantly nauseated by the mere mention of it. I bit down on my back teeth to stifle the scream. My entire life seemed like a lie and now they wanted me to tell the truth, all of it, to a bunch of strangers, some of whom were still twitching from the DTs. I couldn't do it. I wouldn't do it. They couldn't make me, surely?

"I hear you like writing," Anton added. "Just think of it as writing a story. Just yours."

Manipulative bastard.

CHAPTER 39

The Big Bad Wolves

My eyes shot open. I gasped for air. Had I been screaming? I was gripping the sheets on either side of me in both hands. Sweat poured down the side of my face, down my neck, my chest. My pyjamas were wet all over, my pants sticking to my legs. I looked over at Lisa, who was snoring loudly. The screams had either been in my head or she had snuck Valium in again.

The dream, the terror, was always the same.

I am sitting on the floor in the middle of a small room. I am a young and old version of myself. The room is made entirely of glass, including the ceiling. It is dimly lit, but I don't see the source of the light and I can't see anything beyond the glass cube. I pull myself up from the floor and go to touch one of the walls, then run to another and when I reach the third, a huge black shaggy wolf leaps up at me against the glass on the other side. He is on his hind legs and taller than me, snarling, pawing, scratching and snapping at the glass. I jump back, terrified. I realise I am bleeding from somewhere. The white dress I'm wearing is starting to soak through with my own blood. The mangy, rabid wolf is joined by another, then another; then there are four, all identical, all pushing up against the glass wall, howling, yelping maniacally, threatening to break through. I run to the fourth wall and they follow. I run my hands along the glass only to find a sliding door – and it's open. I panic. I can't decide whether to run out into the blackness or try to close the door. But it's too late … I'm backed up into the far corner of the room as they enter it, growling, sniffing the air, all four ready to attack.

Four wolves.

My four perpetrators.

My subconscious was drawing me out of my denial and suppressed memories in a violent and inconvenient way. I was starting to remember.

Four perpetrators. Two childhood molesters, one adolescent rapist, one adult rapist.

Motherfucker, I was starting to remember.

The next morning, Lisa decided she was RHT-ing. Refusing Hospital Treatment. Leaving against the recommendations of the staff. But she wasn't going quietly. Inconsiderate bitch. It was my Life Story day. I was supposed to have read it already but the staff had spent the morning behind closed doors with her, trying to convince her to stay in treatment. Then they had pulled us all into the Group room and tried to get us to convince her that she should choose recovery over crack.

"Don't go," I had urged. I had begun to really like Lisa. Rehab makes for strange bedfellows.

"It's not worth it," added Stacey.

"Fuck you!" she spat.

A few minutes later, she was stuffing her clothes and expensive knee-length boots into suitcases, huffing and puffing dramatically, throwing her hands up in the air, shouting, "Fuck recovery" and "I made more money as a whore." All sentiments I agreed with in principle but couldn't verbalise – certainly not in the environment I found myself.

I sat on the edge of my bed, clutching the printed copy of my life story I had been holding onto all morning in anxious anticipation of reading it to the group. The corners of the pages were curling in my sweaty palms and, out of pure anxiety, I had kept dropping the pile of papers and having to reorganise and reshuffle them. My life story, like my life, was a mess.

For some or other reason, Anton had given me permission to use the facility's computer to type it as opposed to handwriting it, which everyone else had to do. The Recovery Assistant, Robbie, had overseen me in the evenings, but he had left me alone for long periods at a time so I'd gone through the centre's hard drive looking for confidential information. Robbie was too trusting and too cute too be an RA. One of the inmates, Dale, had called me "Special and Different" when he found out I had been allowed special privileges. I had told him to "Get fucked."

It was the first thing I had written in years and I pulled out all the stops. I found my words again and they were big, beautiful words.

I'd read and re-read it about 20 times and edited it about 20 times more than that. I felt slightly nauseated – there was shit in there that I'd never told a living soul.

I read through it again.

The slimming tablets at 17, then the LSD and the weed and the alcohol. The pills, speed and more alcohol when I was overseas. Coming back home to find Cape Town shmangled to the hilt on Ecstasy and diving head first right into that culture. Then the coke and more pills, the buttons and more coke, the crack and then the heroin. Oh, and some tik and lots of pharmaceuticals thrown in along the way. And that was just my drug grocery list.

My life was a B-grade movie.

The eating disorder. The self-harm, the promiscuity, the toxic relationships, the blackouts, the multiple overdoses, the prostitution. And the sexual abuse that was now inconveniently resurfacing.

It was a life gone wrong. I had kept spinning, spinning out of control, fuelled solely by my own desire for self-destruction. The papers were vibrating on my trembling lap. Was I really going to reveal all that to them, these strangers? I felt unbelievably nauseous. I dropped the pages and once again they scattered onto the bedroom floor as I ran to the en suite bathroom just in time to vomit in the toilet bowl. I wrapped my arms around the toilet and rested my head on it, breathing deeply.

"Desiree!" I heard Sydney's voice at the door, followed by a firm knock. "Life Story time!"

I wiped the puke from my lips with the back of my hand, exited the en suite bathroom and glanced over at Lisa, who was still packing her clothes and denial into her bags.

"Bye, Lisa. Take care of yourself please. Stay in touch." Everybody said that in rehab but nobody really meant it.

Deep breath. Shit was about to get real.

CHAPTER 40

Control Freaks

"My name is Desiree, and I am an addict."

"Desiree," the group responded.

I still struggled intensely with that introduction. I didn't feel like an addict.

The evidence, of course, indicated that I was an addict, but I didn't feel like I had a drug problem; lots of other problems, yes, but drugs just helped me deal with them. I wasn't convinced that that made me an addict.

We were back in Group session. Stacey had set the tone, explaining how she had phoned her mother for help when she hit rock bottom despite having destroyed that relationship, and others were relating to her story with their own tales of pleas for help and obliterated relationships. I was the only one who hadn't spoken and suddenly I felt multiple pairs of eyes come to rest on me, urging me to speak.

Silence.

Fuck, I hated these silences.

Heavy, loaded, awkward, anxious silence. The pulling, knotty sensation in my stomach compelled me to end it.

"I phoned my dad." More silence.

Damn it.

"From a payphone down the road from my house."

"God, you actually have a dad?" asked Dale. "Lucky you. What did you say to him?" He was such an ass-kissing, self-absorbed-wannabe-counsellor.

I leaned back on the rear legs of the chair, balancing on my toes. "I said, 'I'm in trouble. Darren has been arrested. He's gone now and I'm all alone. We've been using heroin. Please come get me.'"

Anton leaned forward slightly in his chair. "What did Darren get arrested for?"

I looked back over my shoulder, out of the small sash window.

"Honestly, I don't know. He disappeared with Cliff, his dodgy racist friend, for a few days and then came back and was all agitated and he had an electronic cash register that we tried to sell on Sea Point Main Road. The next day, there were two overweight Afrikaner cops from somewhere on the Garden Route arresting him at the house. He told me to get some smack and drive up to fuck-knows-where and bring it to him and to phone his parents. Then they left. I had no money, just enough for that phone call. I just couldn't any more."

Anton nodded, leaning back again. "Do you see how that is an example of your powerlessness?"

I had no idea what he was talking about but nodded anyway.

"Powerlessness," I repeated, for effect, "Sure."

Whatever.

Stacey and I were sitting at the bottom of the sloped garden, nearly in the flowerbed, chain smoking and pushing the burned-out filters into the soil surrounding the fynbos. The sun beat down and I felt the warmth in my bones for the first time in days. Stacey had rolled up the sleeves of her top – something she never did – and stretched her arms out, palms turned up toward the sun.

"That's fucked up." She lit another cigarette from the one she had just finished. "So you never saw him again?"

I extinguished my cigarette in the cloddy dirt and leaned back on my hands.

"Kinda. My dad phoned his parents and I guess they bailed him out and sent him to a fancy rehab. I went to that shit-hole of a rehab with motherfucking evil-eyed goats. I lasted a few weeks, then got kicked out for 'fraternising'. Then I was on my own, living with my mom, but I didn't have him any more."

Stacey had been rubbing her left forearm with her right hand and, with the tip of her chewed fingernail, was now absent-mindedly outlining the raised welts where scar tissue had formed. "That's a shitty way to end a four-year relationship ..."

I scratched my palms, cursing my allergy to grass, and laughed. "I was invited to his family session, a fucking conjoint, at the rehab! What a joke! I was high as a kite and they were talking about his damages and as though I was the victim, but nothing got resolved. I followed him to my first NA meeting after that. Another joke! I put my hand up for 60 days clean and I had shot up hours before. But, you know what, I liked the applause."

We both laughed and I did a mock bow from the waist to imaginary applause.

"I saw him around Mowbray – his secondary care was there and so were my dealers – but I was using and he was in recovery and I had no idea what recovery was and couldn't understand why he didn't want to be with me any more. I was fucking heartbroken."

"So ... did you just move on?"

"I chose heroin. Oh, and one night at a meeting he told me he had a new girlfriend. The choice had been made for me. It was out of my control."

Stacey lit two cigarettes and handed one to me. I took it and took a long drag. We both sat in silence, looking out over the glen.

"Stace," I asked, "why do you do it?"

"I don't know. I do it because it feels good."

I looked down at her arm and the red welts and criss-cross-stitched scar tissue looked almost vibrant against her pale, freckled skin.

"How can it feel good? You cut yourself. You hurt yourself really badly."

She didn't know I immersed myself in near-boiling water almost daily and was asking more for me than for psycho-educational purposes. She unrolled her sleeves and pulled them back down to her wrists.

"That's why it feels good. It's like any drug. It's better than feeling any real emotion. I hurt myself so that no one else can. It's a fucked-up form of control, but it really is the only one I know that works."

I nodded. I needed to take a bath.

Control. That's all we wanted. That was the only thing we didn't have.

CHAPTER 41

Daughters and Other Whores

My mother was the only one who agreed to come to a conjoint. She was the only one left, if I had to be honest, and the only true remaining victim of the last year of my death-defying addiction. A few weeks ago she was calling me a *jintu* and slapping me across the face; now she was all smiles and politeness and acting as though she had eaten a sedative sandwich before arriving.

"The lies," she was saying, "I just can't handle the lies." She shook her head repeatedly.

She was being painfully polite, wearing her public-people face – and she was excelling, being about as delightful as an all-day breakfast menu. She was dressed impeccably, as always, in a black knee-length skirt and a red-black-and-green striped polycotton long-sleeved shirt that buttoned up the front and ended with a bow at the neck. She had paired it with her signature high heels, which had made it difficult for her to navigate the steep climb up to the house.

Anton nodded.

"What lies aggravated you the most, Beryl?" He addressed her with an unnerving familiarity.

"All of them!" She threw her hands up in the air then remembered herself and returned them to her lap, one elegantly jewelled hand folded over the other. "All of them. About the drugs and where she was getting the drugs, and the stealing!" She shook her head again.

"How much money do you think she has stolen from you?" he asked.

"Thousands." Pause. "Thousands," she replied, emphatically. "But the worst was my mother – her grandmother's – china. She stole that, you know? And sold it. For drugs."

I thought she might shed a tear but, no, she never cried. Ever. Except for that time at the attorney's office during the divorce proceedings when she had dragged my brother and I with to bear witness to my father's malevolent actions. Then she cried, she wailed, and I had never been so frightened in my life. Now I could feel Anton looking at me even though I had become deeply interested in a patch of carpet just in front of my chair.

"How do you feel about all of this, Desiree?"

I looked up at him and glanced over at my mother but could not hold her gaze.

"I feel guilty. I feel awful." Those, I think, were the words they wanted to hear.

Truth was, I actually felt petrified. I had been crapping myself about the conjoint all morning. I didn't care about the things she did know; I was terrified that he was going to tell her all the things she didn't. I knew she wasn't stupid; she had probably guessed and surmised a lot of it, but to have it confirmed would be another story entirely. A few weeks before – when she had found out about the theft of my Ma's antique china – she had been so enraged, I thought she was going to have a heart attack right in front of me.

"You fucking *jintu*!" she had screamed, slapping me across the face, grabbing fistfuls of my hair, tugging at it wildly and then grabbing me by the crotch. "Why don't you sell this rather?" I had stood pushed up against the wall, entirely motionless, numb, allowing her to hit me, knowing I deserved it.

But she was showing none of that anger at the conjoint. No, she was showing the sweet, kind, loving and compassionate codependent side today.

There was no denying it: I had put this woman through a hundred versions of living hell and she had not let go of me. I wasn't entirely sure why and I didn't given it much thought until I had sobered up sufficiently. I tried to formulate her script: Was there a sense of martyrdom? Look at what I have to put up with? I have a junkie, thieving, whoring daughter and I'm the only one standing by and taking the abuse. Did she derive a certain amount of gratification from being the long-suffering mother of an active addict? Was she codependently crazy? Or did she actually love me? I had no answers, but a part of me was grateful that she never gave up on me. But not grateful enough to warrant full disclosure. I did not want her to know about the prostitution or the credit-card fraud or the other thefts. I did not want her to know that I pretended to travel to work by train with her every day and then take the train back to St James to sit on the benches with the trains chugging past behind me and the ocean waves breaking on the rocks in front of me, using all day until it was time to "come home from work". Or that I often sat in Wynberg Library all day, also using, running my hands along the spines of books I would never read and falling asleep in the Reader's Corner or using the computers to google new ways of committing crimes. I did not want her to know that I suspected Darren had broken into her flat and stolen her jewellery. And I didn't want her to know that I had had a key cut to the front door when she had left it lying around or that I had escaped the flat through the garbage hatch. I really did not want her to know that the last time I had come out of rehab I had conned her out of money saying that I owed it to dealers, that my life was in danger if I did not pay it back. I just took the cash – R1200 – and went to use. A lot.

No, I did not want her to know these things. I chewed my bottom lip until I tasted blood. Was he going to tell her?

"Beryl," said Anton. His tone was conclusive. "I believe, and I hope you agree with me, that Desiree needs more time in treatment. She still has a lot to work through and would benefit from at least another month here."

I looked up at him, shocked, licking the tiny droplets of blood from my lips. Another month?

My mother nodded in agreement and laughed nervously, "If that's what you think is best." She turned to me. "If that's what you want?"

I felt trapped, ambushed. And yet strangely relieved. Anton and my mother were discussing arrangements around weekend leave should I decide to stay longer.

I looked up at my mom then at Anton. I wanted this to be over. "Yes, I'll stay another month."

CHAPTER 42

The Last Convincer

Home for the weekend. Four weeks sober. My mind was fucking spinning.

"I'll leave the key here," he said. "Your mom should be home from work in an hour or so."

"Thank you, Jonathan," I hugged him. "I'll see you later for the meeting." I closed the front door behind him and ran across the open-plan lounge to the balcony to watch him leave.

I picked up the keys. Looked up at the wall clock. My mind was resolute. There was no debate. I had one and a half hours. I raced to the phone and, as if on autopilot, punched Adbul's number into the keypad.

He was surprised to hear my voice. "Baby, where've you been?"

"Joburg. I missed you. Please come."

"Ten minutes," and he disconnected.

I had no money so this was going to be our usual exchange. I stripped down to my panties and threw on a purple satin gown. And waited. Fifteen minutes of watching the second hand travel around that godforsaken wall clock. I decided that sober-anxious was way worse than withdrawing-anxious. The door buzzer finally rang. I jumped up, ran to the door and pressed the intercom button, scooping up the keys to unlock at the same time. He was at the door in record time and I let him in.

"You got fat," he assessed me, bluntly. I didn't respond.

"Where you really been? The rehab?"

"It doesn't matter, Adbul." I hugged him and planted a kiss on his cheek. He still smelled the same. Like my dirty, dangerous past.

"You got the stuff?"

He held the quarter up in his right hand just out of my reach.

"You know, sex first."

Fuck.

I led him to my bedroom, shrugged off my gown and pushed my panties to the floor. He unbuckled his belt, then his jeans and then, too roughly, pulled me close to him, kissing my neck.

"I missed you."

"I missed you too, baby," I lied.

"Why d'you leave me?" he gripped my forearms tightly, painfully.

"You … you're hurting me," I whimpered.

It all happened so quickly. He spun me around, pushed my shins against the base of the bed, spreading my legs apart with his knees. He pushed my back, my face, down into the bed and with his other hand forced his huge penis inside my asshole. I screamed into the duvet as he entered me without restraint. Utter disbelief lit up my skin, my bones, my mind.

I was being sodomised.

Over and over again, the excruciating tearing and stretching of my insides. I wrapped my teeth around my own hand and bit down hard. I started dry heaving and sobbing but I did not protest.

God, grant me the Serenity … God, grant me the Serenity …

When it was finally over, he withdrew and dropped the quarter on the bed next to my face. Buckling up his jeans, he promised to "see me soon" and I heard him walk down the passage and let himself out. I lay on the bed, throbbing in unbearable pain, staring at the tear-shaped plastic quarter of heroin inches from my tear-stained face. They had said in rehab that when you find recovery, if you relapse you don't start over again, you just pick up where you left off. They were wrong. This was way worse than where I left off.

I slowly got up off the bed, pulled on the gown, rummaged through the drawer next to the bed and found an old bankcard. I limped to the kitchen, not caring about the blood and semen droplets leaving a messy trail behind me. I found a straw in the kitchen drawer and cut it to size, then cut the quarter open and poured some of the white-grey powder out onto the kitchen counter and shaped it into a line with the card, wishing I had kept an old syringe.

I considered not doing it. Just for today.

Fuck it. I was on weekend leave. I was going back to rehab on Monday anyway.

Last time.

Really.

Last time.

Promise.

CHAPTER 43

The Good Girl

Despite the core principle of honesty in the 12-step programme, I kept my weekend relapse and rape a secret. For some inexplicable reason, I managed to avoid the mandatory drug test when I returned that Monday. I had done everything else they asked of me, but I was taking that secret to the grave. I stayed an extra two months and was compliant and obedient ... the perfect patient.

I found Farahnaaz, an amazing, caring, militant sponsor – a combination of Mary Poppins and Hitler, who beat me relentlessly with the recovery stick. Farahnaaz was the first woman with whom I developed any kind of meaningful and trusting relationship and – considering I despised most other women – that was an impressive achievement on her part. She made me do written step work until my fingers were numb while I waited for the promised "spiritual awakening" – my own personal blinding white light on the mountain top – as I had been through the 12 steps twice already. I didn't get it. I felt robbed, but I persevered, sullenly in private and enthusiastically in public.

I asked Farahnaaz's advice and moaned to her listlessly almost every day.

"I feel like I'm dying!" I would complain over the telephone.

"You just feel like that; you're not actually dying. This too shall pass." Which made me want to vomit but it was nevertheless strangely reassuring. Because I did not trust my own judgement one iota, I ran every decision by her.

Should I be interviewed by a magazine featuring women in recovery?

No.

Should I keep living with my mom?

Yes.

Coke or Fanta?

Coke Light.

I attended more than the prescribed 90 meetings in 90 days, sometimes hitting three meetings a day just to stay sober on that given day. It was undeniable overkill, but I was desperate to cling to my shaky sobriety whether I wanted to sink back into sweet oblivion or not, which was most days.

In the early days, those following that atrocious reunion, Abdul had returned to my mother's flat, gained access to the corridor outside our flat and thrown two quarters through the crack in the open kitchen window. I panicked. It was *right there*. I scooped them up, held them in my sweaty palm, then tossed them back out the window and told him to "Fuck off!" I was wearing the purple satin gown in which he'd raped me. As I buzzed the intercom to let him out of the driveway gate, I stripped down to my underwear, ran to my room and stuffed the shiny, shame-drenched gown into the back of the cupboard.

I had found a home group in both Narcotics Anonymous and Alcoholics Anonymous, meetings I attended regularly and faithfully, where I made friends and found mentors. To inject more spirituality into my recovery, I even travelled out of town for NA and AA conventions. I did service at meetings, which often meant being the Coffee Bitch, providing the attendees with cheap coffee, tea and biscuits. They called it "the most important service position" because addicts can be grouchy fuckers if they don't get coffee and biscuits, the highlight of most meetings for some. I would also promote the literature and talk to newcomers about the books and the pamphlets. Or I would chair the meetings, my own personal favourite, upfront and centre – in charge.

I joined subcommittees to help other addicts, answering calls and meeting people at meetings and doing "12 Step calls", telling my story to alcoholics still deep in the throes of delirium tremens with half a hope that they would find encouragement in my inflated story.

By the time I was six months clean, I was sponsoring a legion of six young girls. I collected my sponsees like trophies and filled my weeks shouting at them about how they would die if they relapsed, all the while trying to be patient and loving and wise.

I had worked on my dysfunctional relationship with food and my body image.

It wasn't a wholesale success, but my food had stopped conversing with me, which was at least progress. I gained the customary weight one does when you stop spiking heroin every day – and realised that 41 kilograms of skeletal junkie with track marks was not as chic a look as I had once thought. I no longer felt the need to submerge myself in near-boiling water.

I had seen a psychiatrist, Dr Greg MacCarthy, sat cross-legged on his armchair and had lied to him. He, however, had some experience with my type and slowly helped me manage my intense and fluctuating moods, my irrational rage and PTSD, by restraining me properly in a comfy chemical straightjacket. We figured out the PTSD in about session four when I complained about the levels of my anxiety. He dropped a bunch of keys on his desk and I nearly shot straight out of the chair. I gave him marks for showmanship and went to fill the script for anxiolytics. He used fancy terms like "attachment disorder" and "affect regulation".

What I understood was that I needed to learn my feeling words. And that "fuck you" was not a feeling. My mother did not understand this need for medication. She scoffed at the fistfuls of money I passed over to psychiatrist and pharmacist alike.

"Surely you're fixed now?" she asked derisively one day.

Fixed? I felt even more broken than ever. But I walked away silently, closed my bedroom door and wept for our still-fractured relationship.

I was even working as the administrator at the rehab where I got sober. A few weeks after I was discharged, Anton had called to ask whether I wanted to answer the phones at the new premises. I had been finding it more than a little difficult to secure any job interviews, what with the massive gaping hole in my CV, so I agreed. And as the centre's needs grew, three days turned into a full time job; and I went from answering phones to doing just about everything. *Everything.* I was completely out of my depth, but I had efficiency, autodidactic skills and over-compensation on my side.

Akron House offered treatment to those who could not afford the hefty price tag that came attached to other private rehabilitation centres. We helped those who could not find recovery elsewhere. We literally took in the unwashed, addicted masses, sometimes at a huge rebate, sometimes free of charge. It felt good to be working in the addiction recovery field. It felt gratifying to be helping others like myself. You only keep what you have by giving it away, the programme told me.

Both the Fellowship and Farahnaaz told me to stay out of a relationship for at least the first year and it had been nearly two – and, being the good little recovery soldier I was, I diligently complied. Not for lack of advances or attractions, but for fear of self-implosion. I couldn't bear the thought of someone hurting me, rejecting me, abandoning me or even loving me. I kept my distance, marked out my imaginary solo dance space, staying single and celibate along with the other early-recovery compulsive masturbators, caffeine junkies, chain smokers and comfort eaters.

I was the perfect recovering addict. "Captain Recovery" is what I was often called, though not always in flattery. I didn't mind; I had a newfound sense of purpose. Recovery was what I did now. And I had to do it perfectly, although most days it felt like I was dying a slow, emotional death, agonising over my lost love and struggling to navigate this new anaesthetic-free life. After meetings most nights, I sat in the passenger seat of the VW Golf of my friend, Adam, both of us lamenting our inability to regain any sense of normalcy. Happy, joyous and free, they promised. The wounded children that Adam and I were wailed about the injustice and pain of yet another broken vow.

One mid-winter evening, I was chairing a meeting, holding recovery court, at the Observatory Community Centre. I was 22 months clean and sober. I was wearing my favourite scarf. I loved that scarf. It was thick and woollen, predominantly bold, bright red but trailing off into hues of blue and green and yellow. It was long and luxuriously soft and could easily be wrapped around my neck and shoulders three, maybe four times. I wore it every day and night that winter, the thick rolls pushing my auburn curls up around my ears.

I sat up front in the crowded, stuffy hall, already reading the introductory preamble, when I saw him, Robert. He had come in late, shuffling down the back row – or 'Denial Aisle', as it was commonly known, to find a seat. Even from that distance, I managed to dispatch a disapproving look. He responded with a sheepish, charming grin. I had met Robert before at a Stepping Stones Open Day a few months prior and during our brief exchange he had made me laugh. That was quite an accomplishment because I took My Recovery Very Seriously.

That evening in Obs, he responded to the share and made everyone laugh with his take on "thinking he hadn't had a drug problem but a financial problem". I saw him put his hand up for nine-months-to-one-year during the clean-time countdown. Damn. He was a relative newcomer. An untouchable.

After the meeting, he came on over. He had a thrown-together look about him; street urchin-cross-welfare recipient but he wore it strangely well. His dark hair – in stark contrast to his pale skin – was over-gelled and he wore glasses that gave him a nerdish allure. He stood disarmingly close to me.

"Sorry I was late," he adjusted his spectacles, pushing them back up the bridge of his nose. They slid down again almost immediately. "I really like your scarf," he continued, fingering the tassels.

I couldn't speak.

Every part of my being felt magnetically pulled to his.

I never wanted to move again.

PART 5

Bending the Rules

CHAPTER 44

13th Stepping

My relationship with Robert started dishonestly. Despite the fact that he had hooked up with a friend of mine, I still pursued him doggedly. He didn't ward off my unsubtle advances and it wasn't long before we were shamelessly flirting. He hadn't yet cracked a year's clean time, but I was obsessed with him.

He was charming, smart and witty. He had a constant nervous energy about him that excited and aroused me. The developing relationship was drenched in *déjà vu*: I was once again attracted to the *idea* of a person and that romanticised notion of love. Weirdly, like Darren ... Darren all over again. It was also spurred on by the fact that both our sponsors emphatically told us that it was a Very Bad Idea. Tell an addict not to do something and they'll do it. Tell two addicts not to do something and, well, it was a *fait accompli*. I found myself morphing into who it was I thought he wanted me to be: funny, sexy, smart, attentive, loving. He made me feel all those things too and mirrored my aggressive flirtation.

A wise recovery friend warned me: relationships that start dishonestly usually end dishonestly. I scoffed at the idea. We were both in recovery, working on ourselves and our issues. Wasn't that enough? The irony that we were behaving dishonestly, which contradicted the foundation of the programme, was lost on me. The admonitions and sincere warnings made it even more exhilarating, this forbidden love of ours. We didn't give a continental fuck. We were knee-deep in secret trysts and obsessive-compulsive behaviour, only this time all parties present were stone-cold sober. I loved him and he loved me and fuck the world and all the rules that were being foisted on us. Rules like, "Don't get into a relationship within the first year" ... In hindsight it should really be "the first decade". They did say, "Don't get into a relationship with someone under a year if you have more clean time than them." They called that '13th Stepping' in 12-step programmes: the unwritten extra step – widely known and very rarely adhered to. It was regarded as predatory behaviour, taking advantage of an emotionally vulnerable newcomer. Robert was also six years my junior, but he seemed to have no problem being taken advantage of, especially sexually.

I found sex – after a lengthy period of reclaimed celibacy – both profoundly pleasurable and deeply traumatic. I had frequent flashbacks of my adult sexual assaults and, after shagging, would often end up sobbing and shaking. I clearly hadn't dealt with any of my past trauma, but I didn't allow that to get in the way of giving Robert what I thought he wanted, what I thought I had to in order to make him love me more. Robert's response to these episodes was caring and compassionate. I was clearly not the first broken girl he'd been with. He came with his own excess baggage, of course, but I convinced myself that this was different because he was in recovery so surely he wasn't *that* broken. And, besides, if there was any damage, I could fix it. So I gritted my teeth and fed his sexual appetite. My approach obviously worked: he wanted me and, more importantly, he stayed.

We moved in together within a few months of hooking up. Everybody thought that was also a terrible idea. We had nothing except the income from our low-paying jobs – he was a chef at a popular restaurant in Observatory – and a red bucket. A friend had given us the bucket as a housewarming present and it was the first and only new thing we owned as we moved our few belongings into a gorgeous renovated two-bedroomed apartment in Muizenberg. Robert's father was a much-loved minister in the Methodist Church and his mother worked in the finance department at a private school in Somerset West. They were good people and – despite questioning the move we were making – they bought us a bed, some appliances and a few other things essential to not living like paying squatters. I borrowed money from friends for the deposit and first month's rent. We channelled our combined addict determination and energies into getting what we wanted. And, as in active addiction, we got it whether it was good for us or not.

We played at being grown-ups. We were really good at submerging ourselves in our collective denial, particularly around our ability to support ourselves financially and around the maintenance of a relationship that tenuously held two very fractured individuals.

Robert worked the long hours and days required of a chef so he only had one day off every two weeks or so. Very quickly, I began to feel lonely and deeply abandoned. I wasn't getting enough love or attention. I was needy. I was terrified. I wanted more and so I became demanding, hauling out the old "How much do you love me?" tests and administering them constantly and consistently.

"Do you love me?" I would ask, incessantly.

"Yes," he would reply, trying to quell my rising insecurities.

"How much?"

"More than I've loved anyone."

I didn't believe him. He was beginning to sound tired. I felt unlovable, even within the bounds of our relationship. My childhood abandonment issues reared their ugly two-faced heads. I still didn't feel good enough. I still wasn't sure if he'd stay or leave.

By now I was training as an addictions counsellor at Akron House, facilitating the morning groups and running occasional full-day Inner Child workshops – all while, as its coordinator, still making sure the entire place ran smoothly under hugely difficult circumstances. The treatment centre's policy of offering affordable (or sometimes free) treatment came at a huge cost to the staff. We started being paid short or very late. Also, the centre's director, Anton, who suffered excruciating cluster headaches, was hardly around any more, which was not ideal. I felt a huge sense of responsibility for making things work in his absence. I was in a full-blown codependent relationship with my former counsellor. Over the years, he had stepped up into a much sought-after paternal role. He had helped me beyond measure to find hope and to find sobriety. He even paid for me to start seeing a therapist, for work supervision purposes, but we both knew I needed help on a much deeper level. I felt hugely indebted to him and once again I had to be the proverbial "good daughter" to my incidental guardian. I felt deeply defensive of him (the lengthy nonappearances on short notice, the late salary payments) and, at the same time, hugely conflicted.

But I needed to pay rent and continue playing house with my also-absent partner whom, I soon discovered, had a predilection for flirting, needing constant affirmation from other women. It caused huge, histrionic arguments and pervasive paranoia. He insisted it was harmless, swore blind that he would never do it again. I wanted to believe him – and he was so convincing at making me do just that. So, I did what any lonely, savagely insecure 30-year-old woman in my predicament would do. I decided it was time to have a baby.

We sat facing one another on the hand-me-down, brown sofa he had bought from an ex-employer.

"I think we should have a baby," I stated. It wasn't really a question. I had given it a lot of thought – obsessively, in fact – and had run through how the conversation should play out. The result was that I unilaterally decided that it was going to become a reality.

"A baby?" His face drained, went even paler than it usually was, which was practically translucent on any given day. "But we've only been together for six months."

"But I want a baby."

"I'm 24 years old. I don't think I'm ready for that yet."

"But I'm 30 and I think it's the right time for me."

He shifted his position, resting his elbows on his knees and clasping his hands together tightly in front of him. The ensuing silence was unbearable. I wouldn't be able to stomach it if he didn't agree with my decision. This is what I wanted. It would fix everything.

"Okay," he blurted out, suddenly. Beads of perspiration had formed on his hairline. "When d'you want to start trying?"

"Is that a yes?" I smiled. I knew it was.

"Yes, let's have a baby." He slumped back onto the couch. "I want to start trying as soon as possible."

It was November. I stopped taking the pill the next day. Robert and I had sex even more frequently – which he didn't seem to mind – but my focus was fixed. I gritted my teeth through every act of goal-driven intercourse, horrific flashbacks pushed to the outer regions of my awareness, willing that one triumphant sperm to connect miraculously with one ovum. I even downloaded an app on my phone to tell me when my window period for ovulation would be. To increase my chances of conception, I started subtly scheduling sex. I was obsessed. I had never wanted anything more in my life. Except maybe when I'd wanted heroin.

CHAPTER 45

And Baby Makes Three

I'm pregnant. I'm pregnant. I'm pregnant.

I repeated it over and over in my head. I played with alternatives. *I am expecting. I am with child.*

Really? Jesus, where were we? Medieval times?

I'm pregnant seemed apt. It was the truth, my new reality. *I'm expecting* left too much open to intolerable responses.

Expecting what? Excitement? Compassion? Love?

It was a bad idea to hold any such expectation. The past had proven this. Lower your expectations and avoid disappointment. Yet here I was hoping to achieve a different outcome. I should have known better, but I didn't. Stupid me.

Yes, stupid, ungrateful, naïve me.

Noxious fear churned in my stomach. How should I do this? Blurt it out? Or make small talk and then make the grand announcement?

I clenched my teeth. What was I going to say again? Oh right, *I'm pregnant.*

I rubbed my tummy where my fear and my baby lay. My baby. I was going to be a mother. He was going to be a father. I knew I would make a good mother, or at least one that did not actively damage her child. I would do my best. I would love him or her with all that I had. And that would be good enough.

But, first, I had to break the news. Bile rose up and threatened to choke me. I had to say it – or risk not saying it at all.

"I'm pregnant."

My mother looked up from her crossword puzzle, dragged on her cigarette, then blew the smoke across the room at me.

"Pregnant?" she snorted. "Now why would you go do something so fucking stupid?"

I hung my head, ashamed. I felt like a knocked-up teenager. I was 30 years old and living with the father of my child.

* * *

We told everyone – family and friends – that it was all completely unplanned. A joyous, unexpected miracle. I didn't want anyone thinking we had purposefully made such a foolish decision.

This pregnancy was, however, by no means my first. I had been consistently careless and reckless. This behaviour had resulted in a few (grateful) miscarriages and, at the age of 22, an abortion that was absolutely necessary because the father never knew of the pregnancy and also happened to be in a long-term relationship at the time. But this child ... this child I wanted and I crossed my fingers and prayed that my war-zone of a womb would see this one through to the end.

I had to come off my psychiatric meds as soon as I found out I was pregnant and my psychiatrist inconveniently immigrated to Canada around the same time. I became certifiably mad again. Madness and pregnancy were not a good combination. Madness and anything usually isn't. I truly thought that a baby would fill an emotional void, that I would be made whole by motherhood, that it would fix a relationship that was showing massive cracks in its already shaky foundation. Instead, I felt resentment towards the growing foetus that took over my entire being. It felt like a violation, a re-enactment of *Invasion of the Body Snatchers*.

I was violently sick all the time. There was no morning sickness; there was all-day and all-night nausea and projectile puking. It became so severe that one day I fractured a rib while retching over my mother's toilet. I developed high blood pressure and low blood pressure. I gained an inordinate amount of weight from water retention and also from eating prawns and fresh cherries and other strange food combinations Robert was sent to gather and deliver to his constantly ravenous pregnant girlfriend. Of course, it helped that he worked at a restaurant so most of my calorific needs were both delicious and free. I was eating for two. Hell, I was eating for seven. Unsurprisingly, my body dysmorphia reared its ugly head and I could no longer bear to look at myself in the mirror. You're allowed to gain weight when you're pregnant, I thought. You fat, ugly, gluttonous pig, I added.

And then I developed severe bronchitis, then crippling pleurisy, coughing, hacking incessantly and losing bladder control in the process. I hadn't quit smoking – I refused to let the growing child take cigarettes from me. So I smoked and peed my way through the first part of my third trimester. It was humiliating. I felt physically and emotionally degraded. I never had the pregnancy glow that the books suggest.

My madness was untethered. One day, I decided to cut my hair off simply because it was irritating me. So there I stood in the shower and flipped my wet hair forward and hacked indiscriminately at my curly locks with a pair of blunt kitchen scissors. Robert found me naked, curled up on the floor of the shower, sobbing, with half of my hair clumped around the shower drain. He remained unnervingly calm and fixed what he could of the monumental mess I had made. He was also calm when he found my neatly folded pyjamas in the fridge and when I misheard him and thought he had said he was leaving me and wailed uncontrollably in the car and also when I threatened to kill him for eating the last slice of creamy milk tart that "my mommy had given to me, you cunt!"

The baby was due on 24 September but by August I had had more than enough. Clearly, Isabella knew it and on the evening of 20 August, while I was watching *Desperate Housewives*, I went into distinct, painful premature labour. Calmly, I phoned Mowbray Maternity Hospital and asked what to do. They, equally calmly, told me to time the contractions, which I did while they stayed on the line. They were less than two minutes apart. They advised me to get to the hospital as soon as possible. I phoned Robert at work.

"The baby is coming," I said, trying to hide the mixed emotions of relief and trepidation in my voice. I rechecked my hospital bag, which had been ready, at the front door, for over a month.

Robert made the drive from Observatory to Muizenberg in 12 minutes and, by the time he pulled up outside, was beyond frantic. We drove to the hospital in silence. I knew she was coming. I knew it would all soon be over and I would reclaim myself, my body. It was close to midnight when they did the internal exam and hooked me up to foetal monitors.

"You're going to have the operation now," announced the clearly exhausted young doctor.

"For what?"

He looked at me as though I was as mad as I actually felt.

"To have your baby. She's in foetal distress. We have to do an emergency C-section."

As though I had a choice.

As with most important events in one's life, Isabella's birth flashed by in a blur of hazy recollections. I remember them inserting the spinal needle into the wrong vein and it felt as though my kneecap was going to explode. I remember my body going cold, dead from the anaesthetic. I remember it feeling like someone was vigorously doing the dishes inside of my stomach. I remember wondering – as I had done so many times before and during the pregnancy – what colour she would be. I remember seeing the guarded horror on Robert's sweaty face as he watched from behind the screen they had put up to protect me from seeing my own surgical decimation. And I remember Paul McCartney and Michael Jackson's 'The Girl Is Mine' playing on the radio in the theatre just as I heard three tiny, polite coughs and what sounded like a little lamb bleating.

The girl had been born … and she was mine.

CHAPTER 46

Mommy Blues

The child, as beautiful as she was, all lily-white skin and big brown eyes, did not fill the abysmal void as I had hoped she would. Neither did she fix my relationship with Robert. Or my relationship with my mother, who I thought would be proud of me and become a present and willing grandmother to her grandchild. On the contrary, it gave her more to criticise when we visited.

"The child isn't dressed warmly enough."

"The child is dressed too warmly."

"The child shouldn't be taken out in this weather."

"You're holding the child all wrong."

The child, the child. It became all about the darling child and my flaws as a mother were highlighted in the same way my flaws as a daughter had been.

It was a lot to ask of a helpless infant – especially a premature one who had to be fed with a dropper in the first week of her life – but I despised the fact that her arrival didn't change anything on any deep or significant level.

I soon discovered that I was not a bottomless well of maternal love either. I loved her, of course, but in a detached, curious kind of way. I loved her soft porcelain skin, the sweet smell of the top of her head, her tiny fingers grasping my index finger, the way she attached so effortlessly to her father, which seemed to make him happy. But I hated that she was so needy and dependent and that – because of Robert's continued crappy working hours despite changing jobs – I was often alone with her, locked up in the flat for weeks at a time. None of my other friends had babies or children so I had no one with whom I could relate or complain. They visited and offered what support they could. My friend, Adam, even took Isabella and I to an NA meeting and everyone thought the kid was his. We had a lot of explaining to do that afternoon. But I felt utterly alone in this new role. I also didn't want anyone to know that I was failing at bonding with my baby, that I was not the perfect mother. That I was failing at something I had obsessively created was a devastating blow to my fragile psyche.

As a result, I became an 'admin mom', making sure that she was fed, her nappies were changed, that she slept and she was bathed. I did my best to ensure the basics were covered. But her greedy suckling on my engorged breasts drained my energy – and what felt like my very will to live – like a vampire. I had thought I would reclaim my body after the birth but it was still all geared towards nourishing and nurturing her.

I became bitter, resentful and depressed. I raged, alone, and at Robert. He reminded me that having a baby had been my idea and I raged even more. One afternoon I found myself, in the kitchen in a kind of trance, holding one of Robert's big chef's knives firmly in my hand, unsure of who I was going to slice the blade into. I phoned my therapist and she talked me down calmly and compassionately, explaining that I was suffering from post-natal depression and needed help. I thanked her for intervening in a near-fatality but insisted I was fine. I just had the 'Mommy blues'. It would pass.

After four months, I went back to work and took the child with me. We had no money for daycare and Anton suggested I bring the baby to work with me for a few months. I jumped at the chance. I need to work again. I needed a fixed focus other than the baby and my growing suspicions that Robert was not just flirting with but actually fucking someone else. So I took the innocent infant to the rehab centre filled with toxic addicts and alcoholics and didn't think that perhaps it was not the best place for her. Up until this point, it had been all about her, but now I needed this for myself. So when I returned and was promoted to the position of addictions counsellor, I convinced myself that I had made the right decision. I could help people again. I could be productive and efficient and compassionate. To make up for my obvious failings as a mother, I could excel at something else. I could go back to the safety of Akron House and end my self-imposed isolation. I would feel needed and indispensable again.

But as a full-time addictions counsellor I was, once again, way out of my depth. My lack of formal qualifications made me feel inadequate. I had a natural ability with people, especially other addicts, but the rest I made up as I went along. I was assigned my first clients and in one-on-one sessions and group therapy, I nodded and reflected empathetically at the appropriate times and was entirely engaged in being the one to lead them out of addiction and into the bright, shining light of recovery.

In between sessions, I would breastfeed Isabella in a corner of the women's sleeping quarters, then hand her back to the woman who cooked all the meals and rush off to another group or individual session. I slowly grew in confidence in my work. I was being mentored by Anton (when he was there) and Fonnie, whose approach to counselling was unconventional yet refreshingly authentic.

"I'm not a professional," he would remind me. "I'm a fucking alcoholic helping other alcoholics." I would smile and be grateful for this man who had been so instrumental in my journey to sobriety. I pushed myself to prove that their faith in me had not been misplaced. I did everything by the book, even though I had no actual book to refer to. The work was challenging and I rose to the lofty task. I gave everything I had all while trying to raise an infant in a rehab and still trying my utmost to hold onto the ever-thinning emotional string that tied me to Robert.

As a result of expending all my resources on others and saving nothing for myself, I fell ill. Very ill. Pneumonia. Because I had an eight-month-old baby to consider, I refused to go to hospital. I hated hospitals; people got sicker there every day. They died there. I tried to recover at home but simply couldn't cope with looking after a baby, and Robert couldn't take time off work to look after me. Robert's parents came to fetch Isabella one evening and took her to their home in Somerset West for a few days while I took care of myself. I tried to eat but couldn't. I couldn't even smoke a cigarette, it was that bad. I was pumped full of potent antibiotics and eventually – two weeks later – I started to, quite literally, breathe again.

But that's when the seizures started. At first I thought I had been drugged. It started with sound distortions and seeing rainbow-coloured auras around everything. Then my jaw would shudder and my mouth would open and shut involuntarily. The room, the world, would start to spin and I'd feel like vomiting. The seizures would last for a few minutes and then pass as quickly as they'd come on. I'd be left feeling utterly drained and disoriented. Visits to the doctor and even a professor of Neuroscience at the University of Cape Town could find no medical reason for the sudden onset of these episodes. I wasn't epileptic, they declared. I felt that perhaps I had used just one too many narcotics and really, truly fried my brain. My therapist suggested that they were caused by high levels of anxiety and my need to break with an unendurable reality. I processed her hypothesis … I loved my job, but it had made me sick. I loved Robert, but paranoia and suspicion increasingly overshadowed the sentiment. I loved my child, but I felt I was failing as a parent. I felt I was failing at life. Perhaps my therapist was right? Something needed to change. Almost as soon as I made that realisation – two months and several uncontrollable seizures later – the fits stopped.

I phoned Farahnaaz. "I need to change something drastically."

"Ah, Little …" she said. 'Little' was the abbreviation of her nickname for me, a term of endearment: Little Crazy Pond Scum. I had come up with it because it was how I felt most of the time: crazy and like stagnant pond slime. "Its time."

"For what?"

"Time to work the Coda steps."

Working the steps of Codependents Anonymous was probably the hardest step work of my recovery. It revealed things about myself that I didn't want to know and stripped off layers of bullshit codependent defects. I was horrified at the self-serving traits I had held onto in order to be liked, to be loved, to avoid rejection and abandonment, perceived or real. I identified how super responsible I was for others, how desperate I was for approval, how insincere I was in my dealings with everyone.

Farahnaaz assured me that the steps would be gentle, but she lied. I felt like my body and mind had been dipped in sulphuric acid. I couldn't stand to be in my own skin. I did not like these new revelations and I scrambled to hold onto the only coping mechanisms that had served me, that had ensured my survival to that point. I did not trust the process so I tried to fix myself hastily, fix all my relationships hurriedly.

I focused all my attention and energy on mending my relationship with Robert. On fixing him.

CHAPTER 47

Boxing Day

Robert and I got married. We also found also ourselves saddled with a *real* unplanned pregnancy. We must have conceived the baby on our wedding night because we were married on Human Rights Day, 21 March 2010, and I was pregnant by the end of April. We had gotten engaged on top of Table Mountain in December of 2008; a gallant, romantic act that Robert thought was a huge surprise to me, but I was completely aware of it throughout the planning and eventual execution. Of course, I acted surprised when he went down awkwardly on one knee and asked me to marry him. I even shed a tear. I still had it: I could still act as though my life depended on it. Which in that moment felt as though it – or at least our relationship – did.

The decision to go through with the wedding was a kind of penitence on his part. Exactly a year after our engagement, he had an actual affair – a sexual relationship with a work colleague – and I found out. I discovered the messages on his Facebook Messenger a few days before Christmas 2009 and sent him packing to his parents. Christmas Day saw me crying into my prawn starter at Auntie Sybil's house with two-year-old Isabella asking, "Why you cwying, Mama?"

The understanding I thought I'd receive from my mother was not to be found. I'm not sure why I thought it would.

"Stop crying," she hissed, unsympathetically. "You're making a scene. You're ruining Christmas for everyone."

A few days later, Robert unfurled his sorry ass from his parents' spare bed and came home at my uncertain invitation. He swore blind that he had seen the error of his ways and accepted full responsibility for needing to fix what he had savagely broken. I had thought long and hard about the prospect of raising Isabella on my own and it was not a reality I was prepared to engage with, as much as I had grown to truly love her. So, after a few months, we decided to get hitched. It took me six weeks to organise a beautiful outdoor wedding and reception at the school where Robert's mom worked. I finally got my fairy-tale wedding, poufy white gown and all. Robert's father officiated, Adam gave a speech in his role as Best Man, which I could neither hear nor remember. All I recall is that there was an abundance of prize orchids donated by a friend of Robert's mom and that Diana bought a CD along and we played 'Son of a Preacher Man' by Dusty Springfield and I sang off-key to Robert after we were officially married.

The second pregnancy had the same effect on me as the first. I became emotionally unstable, the constant hormonal surges dictating my moods and erratic behaviour. I felt the invasion start all over again and did not want to be touched by Robert so I warned him that there would be no more sex. He, of course, was not happy with this turn of events. At 20 weeks, we went for the gender scan and were brusquely informed by the X-ray technician that there was no heartbeat.

"The baby is dead," she announced matter-of-factly.

My gynae confirmed the news the next day: the baby had probably died four weeks prior, but cancerous growths in my placenta essentially meant that my body believed it was still viably pregnant for over a month. I had surgery to have the foetus and hideous placenta removed and – after waking up from the general anaesthetic – felt brutally violated all over again. A slow unravelling began in my mind, an all-too-familiar feeling but one that I knew I had no control over. I was angry with Robert because I sensed he was relieved that the baby had died. When I 'uninvited' him to my follow-up appointments with the gynaecologist, he didn't put up a fight. The emotional space between us was widening. I felt like I was falling into an abyss.

Narcissists like to make people believe they are losing their own minds. It is one of the games they play with their codependent hostages. They believe so deeply in their own lies that they make other people doubt their realities and invariably their own sanity. Robert made me feel like I was fucking crazy throughout our marriage. I knew he was cheating again, but I had no substantial proof. Every time I confronted him, he would shrug his shoulders and roll his eyes as though I should get my head checked. I found myself scouring his phone in the dead of night, checking his pockets for telltale signs of infidelity, checking him for any obvious, outward signs of betrayal. I found none. My gut, my finely honed instincts, screamed "Infidelity!" but he kept to his intricately woven fabrication and I slowly began to doubt my own mental wellbeing.

Until Boxing Day.

We were on our way to visit his family somewhere in the Deep South. He had sent a text to his aunt to ask for the exact address and handed me the phone to await a response. The phoned beeped and I read the message. I dropped the phone onto my lap as though it had scalded my hand, then immediately retrieved it. I read the text again. A single bolt of pain shot to my eyeball. I was sure it was an aneurysm. I was going to be sick.

"Stop the car."

"What?"

"Stop the fucking car. Now." I issued the instruction through clenched teeth, a well-rehearsed stage whisper, so as not upset Isabella who was sucking on her old teething toy, one leg dangled out over her car seat. It was 10 am but the heat was already blistering.

He turned left into a side street and mounted two tyres onto the pavement.

"Who is Candice?' I asked. I could feel the tears starting to force their way up behind my eyes. I willed them back into their tear ducts. Not now. Not yet.

"C-Candice?" His eyes widened.

"Yes. Candice. Do you want me to read the message to you?" I held the phone up. My hands began to tremble. "Hi Baby. Merry Christmas. I hope you had a good one. I did, all that was missing was you. I can't wait to see you on Tuesday. I love you. Your girlfriend, Candice."

"Oh, fuck."

"Who is she?"

"I can explain."

"You better fucking believe it. Take me home now. Tell your family we're not coming – and take me home."

I called Adam on the short drive home.

"Did you know?" I demanded, when he answered. "Did you know Robert was having an affair?"

"No. No, I didn't."

"Then please can you come around to the flat and fetch Isabella for a few hours? Robert and I need to talk."

"Sure," he responded. "I'm really sorry, Dezzy."

Once Adam had collected little Isabella, grim-faced and apologetic for a crime he did not commit, I tore into Robert. My interrogation was merciless, but I felt a strong sense of relief that I was on the verge of reaching a truth, a certainty that I had instinctively known, confirmed.

"How long? How long have you been fucking her?" I screamed.

"Since July." His voice was shaky, his arrogance evaporated. He stood in the middle of the lounge, pale and shaking.

"Six fucking months!" I had been right. I felt vindicated, humiliated and destroyed all at once. "Who is she?"

"She works at the bank. In the same building as me."

"So you've been fucking her at work?" I yelled. I didn't care who heard me. I didn't care about anything any more. My chest constricted. I wanted to vomit.

"I'm sorry …" he started, taking a step towards me. He had started crying, but all I felt was pure revulsion.

"Don't!" I raised my hand, indicating for him to stop. To stop crying, to stop apologising, to stop breathing. "Get out. I need time to think."

He collected his keys from the small side table, turned to look at me as he headed for the front door, tears still streaming down his face.

"I'm so sorry."

"Get the *fuck out!*" I screeched until my voice cracked. "Oh, and you'd better phone your parents and tell them how you've destroyed your family."

And so he left, shutting the door quietly behind him. I burst into paroxysms of uncontrollable tears. I was decimated on every level – and I wanted to use: drugs, alcohol, anything to take the feelings away as fast as possible. I picked up my phone and dialled the number of my sponsee, Taryn. She was on the Sea Point promenade with her family.

"I don't meant to bother you," I apologised, "but I just found out that Robert's been cheating on me for the last six months and, if you don't mind, could you come over please, or else I'm going to do something stupid."

She didn't hesitate. "On my way. Don't go anywhere."

I stayed clean that night – and the ones that followed – thanks in part to Taryn's presence and also out of pure pride. I did not want to give Robert the satisfaction of hammering another nail in my emotional coffin. I was determined not to give him that power. He would not take me away from my reality as he had my sanity. And there was Isabella to think of.

"Daddy's going away for a little while," I told her as she sat between us on the same brown couch where the idea of her had been formulated.

"Why?" she asked, looking at him and then me.

"Because Mommy and Daddy are having problems," Robert said. We had rehearsed that line. "And it's nothing you've done, sweetheart."

She scrunched her nose, then looked genuinely relieved as though she too was suddenly liberated from the toxic dishonesty that had invaded our household over the past half-year.

CHAPTER 48

Out on a Ledge

"Mommy ... Mommy ..."

The softly whispered words, insistent as they were, brought me out of my motionless reverie. I looked down to see Bella gazing up at me, wide-eyed but extraordinarily calm. The index and middle fingers of my left hand held a cigarette that was almost entirely ash while the back of my bloodied right hand was being stroked, rhythmically and repeatedly, by my four-year-old daughter's own soft, small hand.

I extinguished the cigarette on the windowsill.

"It's going to be okay. You're going to be okay. It's going to be okay, Mommy," Bella repeated the soothing mantra.

I did not feel okay. The last thing I remembered was a white-hot, frenetic rage that ignited in my stomach and lurched up into my throat, fiery and bilious. My blood had bubbled viciously under the surface of my skin. I had clenched my fist, crushing the tiny reconstructed ceramic teapot in my hand. Why though? Oh shit ... because Bella had remarked that I was "fixing it all wrong".

Bella, in her customary clumsy way, had dropped the ceramic tea set on the kitchen floor; an accident that had irritated me more than was reasonable or rational. I had retrieved the pieces from the floor, and the tube of superglue and a box of matches from the kitchen drawer. Always picking up the fucking pieces, I thought.

This had not been the plan. I was not meant to be raising a four-year-old alone, doing every goddamn thing solo. My finely honed control issues were failing me dismally; I felt very much out of control.

Just weeks earlier, I had sat across from Adam at a coffee shop. He had expressed his "serious concerns", while I sipped a too-weak cup of coffee.

"I'm worried about you."

"I'm worried about me too."

"I've known you for years and I've never seen you like this. The separation ..." I could tell he was choosing his words carefully. "You should see someone. Maybe get something to, you know, help you through this time."

This time. He couldn't even say the word: divorce.

It had been four months since I had made the healthiest decision of my codependent life. I had stood up in the Wynberg magistrate's court and declared that my short-lived marriage was already over due to 'irreconcilable differences'. A synonym for betrayal, for infidelity. I had undertaken to represent myself and researched the fuck out of 'do-it-yourself' divorces. The entire process took eight months and cost less than R400 (including photocopying). But in the past four months – post-divorce – I had felt myself becoming easily overwhelmed and unduly emotional. I was barely eating and hardly sleeping, but still I was functioning like an A-type on overdrive. My mental bandwidth was so broad that, as exhausted as I was, I couldn't stop *doing* things. All the time.

I reluctantly met with psychiatrist Dr Mitchell. Another friend had referred to him as "Sleepy, the Dwarf" because of his penchant for pushing sedatives, as well as his five-foot, four-inch frame. They hadn't mentioned his bulbous nose and the grey-black bouffant, which I suspected may not have been his own hair. He sat across from me, legs crossed at the knee, almost motionless.

"What are your symptoms?"

I pulled out my phone and found the list I had compiled the night before.

"Well, compulsive list-making, for starters." I looked up to meet his impassive face "That was supposed to be a joke …" He seemed distinctly unamused, scribbling on his yellow A4 notepad.

I ran my finger down the screen and read out my observations:

My thoughts race from the moment I open my eyes. I get two to four hours' sleep a night. I see all types of wrong everywhere and my thinking is absolute. I jump to the worst conclusion, the worst-case scenario in everything. Negative, paranoid, obsessive. My moods swing rapidly, mainly between anger and sadness. I have moments of total hope and euphoria. I am ricocheting between different times and spaces and have vivid flashbacks. My thoughts are disconnected; one thought leads me to another that hooks into a feeling that spirals downward rapidly. I am tearful and feel hopeless at times. My motivation and drive is at an all-time low. I have days of not getting out of bed. I'm agitated and restless. I jump from task to task during the day and am easily distracted. My self-talk is critical and hateful. I am also hypercritical of my daughter. I have intrusive thoughts of suicide, nothing major, just swerving into oncoming traffic. Impulsive over-spending. I just bought outdoor furniture and we don't have an outside area. It was on sale; I went back twice to buy four patio chairs. I have great and inspired ideas, start new tasks and don't finish them. I need to appear perfect. I am flighty and forgetful; I lost my bank card, left the handbrake up and locked my keys in the car three times. And when I drive, I feel like I'm inside a video game.

"Oh," I concluded, "and I really want a baby."

I could see him underline something he had written.

"No," he stated, "that's not a good idea." More writing. "I'm going to prescribe a mood stabiliser and an antidepressant and …"

"No, thanks," I interrupted. I shook my head. "No medication."

I left his rooms, sat in my car, sweating – either from the December heat or from the anxiety that had overcome me. I googled the symptoms again. Just as before, my search brought up one clear, undeniable result.

Bipolar Mood Disorder.

"You did it wrong, Mommy." That's all it had taken to crack

my fragile psyche.

And now, here I was, ceramic shards in the palm of my hand and my young daughter talking to me as though negotiating with a psychiatric patient threatening to jump off a ledge.

Everything snapped back into focus.

I would phone the shrink again on Monday.

And I did. I called the shrink and went back to see him. I filled out his illegible prescription for a mood stabiliser and antidepressant. I took them as prescribed. I reconnected with my therapist and went to sessions regularly, vomiting out my feelings in her calm, soothing space. I was determined to take responsibility for myself, my life, for Isabella.

By this stage I was working in an adolescent unit at a private psychiatric facility. Akron House had been sold out from under us to a larger, more financially lucrative treatment centre. Staff members were being paid short or late all the time. The centre's bills for petrol and food had been piling up, unpaid. There was dissension and hostility amongst the embittered staff – some of whom had been recently hired in an effort to save the faltering establishment – and it filtered down to the patient community. Anton and the owner had engineered the sale without consulting the staff, so I duly resigned so that I didn't go down with the sinking ship. As was my pattern, I broke up with Akron House before it could dump me. Anton accepted my resignation all too easily and I later realised that it suited him, because there was simply no money for retrenchment packages. I also later learned that no contributions had been made to the Unemployment Insurance Fund or the South African Revenue Service either. That tarnished all the good work we had done over the five years I had been there and I left the safety of the only real home I had known, the volatile safety of people who had watched me grow up in recovery, and exchanged it for the most difficult work of my career: working with adolescents who were depressed, angry and filled with self-loathing. My kind of people.

I loved the work; it was so rewarding to see young people adopt concepts and run with the changes during our brief four-week interventions. They weren't like the damaged, drug-addled brains of adults who took ages to show any signs of change. But it was draining, too, because teenagers came with angry fistfuls of drama and I found myself dealing with self-harmers who cut so deeply that they required stitches, boys who tried to hang themselves from shower heads with their shoelaces and girls who threw chairs – and themselves – at boys. It triggered so much in the unprocessed parts of myself and made me desperate to fix them, to help them in a way that I hadn't been helped when I really needed it.

Bella and I were closer than we'd ever been, sharing an almost psychic connection. She was a sensitive, beautiful, emotionally generous child and I needed to parent her and be present for her. I was seven years sober and I could not afford to be negligent of my mental health or my recovery.

I hustled hard for my independence and it was unbelievably empowering. I was helping myself, I was helping others. I was exactly where I was meant to be in my life. And it didn't feel like an act, like some role I was playing to please others.

Shit was hard, but shit was real.

CHAPTER 49

Universal Blame Acceptor

Just as everything started falling into place, I was unexpectedly and brutally retrenched from the adolescent unit for not having any formal qualifications or, as they put it, "not being able to bill through medical-aid schemes". It had become all about the money for the big hospital conglomerate. So I decided to go into private practice while working part-time at another sober-living facility. It was a huge risk. I was supporting myself and Isabella, with the exception of the school fees that Robert agreed to pay. But I took a leap of baseless faith and started seeing private clients at a small group-recovery practice called Prospect Hill. I felt almost debilitated by anxiety but pushed through the fear and added Addictions Counsellor in Private Practice to my CV. My practice thrived. I was helping others competently and confidently but on my terms.

"I need your help with a friend of ours." It was my cousin Trevor, calling from Johannesburg. "Do you have time to talk?"

I always had time for Trevor. "Of course. Who is it?"

He hesitated. "It's Lloyd. I don't know what to do, but he needs help."

"Does he want help?" It's the first question you ever ask. Counselling 101.

"I'm not sure ..." Trevor replied.

"What's he using?"

"Crack ..."

"Oh."

"And heroin."

"Oh. Shit."

"He's a mess," Trevor sighed deeply. "He has patches of hair missing; he's lost two of his front teeth."

I laughed despite the gravity of the conversation. "How the fuck did that happen?"

Trevor didn't laugh. "He bit into an ice cream and they broke right off." He continued, sounding even grimmer: "And his face ... it looks like he's gouged pieces of flesh out of his cheeks and his chin."

"He's a picker then."

It was a common obsessive-compulsive-driven effect of using, picking at one's skin to remove imaginary ingrown hairs or squeezing nonexistent pimples. Sometimes there were sharp implements like tweezers involved. Then the wound would scab over and there would be a whole other thing to pick at.

"Where's his family?" I asked.

"Nowhere. They won't be able to help. He lives in a cottage on some friends' premises by himself. That's why I'm calling ..."

I lit a cigarette.

"Firstly," I said, "he needs to want to stop."

"*Eish*."

"I know. Ask him if he wants to. Tell him that you love him and tell him how it's affecting you seeing him like this."

"And then?" I could hear the doubt in Trevor's voice.

"Well," I replied, "he's probably going to want to do it by himself. Go to a doctor and get detox meds and he'll stop for a while but here's the bitch: he'll *suip* himself fucked up."

"Oh."

"*Ja*."

"Call me again when that happens," I urged.

There was a brief silence, then "How do you know it's going to happen?"

"I just do. This may take a while. But I'm here whenever you need to talk."

"Thanks, my darling. Love you."

"Love you too."

I ended the call, extinguished my cigarette and lit another. I said a silent prayer for Lloyd and all the other still-suffering addicts.

Fuck. Why him? While it didn't surprise me when I saw familiar faces from 'the old days' at NA meetings for the first time or being admitted to the rehabs where I worked, I took no pleasure in hearing that old using acquaintances had succumbed to the terrors of active addiction. For a while, I thought I had been the only one, but clearly that wasn't the case.

I had first met Lloyd at the Students' Union at the University of Cape Town when I went with my brother – a BComm student there at the time – to check out varsity life. I was 15 years old and wore black leggings and a blue-and-black checked brushed cotton shirt over a black vest. And my 12 lace-up Doc Martens, of course. I still had braces on my teeth and my hair had been straightened the week before in another attempt to tame the untameable. A chunk of my hair had fallen out as a result of a chemical reaction with the potent relaxer and my oily scalp, but I told everyone I had burned the hair off leaning over a candle. Nevertheless, I wore a red-and-black paisley bandana, folded and tied around my head like an Alice band to hid the offensive bald patch. It was the middle of the afternoon and the Union was packed with students who were probably meant to be in lectures. Lloyd was Trevor's best friend, skinny and blond, with sparkling, mischievous blue-green eyes. I crushed on him the instant we were introduced. I guessed he was 20 or 21 and told him I was 16, as though that would make my jailbait status more acceptable to him. We spoke about books – he liked science fiction, while I was actually attempting to read Dostoyevsky – which he found both surprising and intriguing. I didn't tell him that I was just being a pretentious prat but wanted to seem deep and complex. I knew that he was attracted to me. I also knew that my father and other male cousins would probably beat the shit out of him if he even dared touch me with a 10-foot barge pole. I wanted it, but it was not meant to be.

It was also not meant to be years later when I returned from the UK and met up with him again at The Three Arts. He had a girlfriend. I had a long-distance boyfriend. The chemistry between us was undeniable as we orbited one another for the next year at Trevor's house, where he was always the "get-shit-done" guy, the "go-get-the-shit" guy. He was also known as the UBA or Universal Blame Acceptor. If you caught on *kak* and needed an alibi, Lloyd would shoulder the blame. He did this because he didn't really care what people thought and also because it was very difficult to get or stay angry with him. One night, at Dulverton Road, we were schnarfed up, locked in deep conversation in the double doorway that connected the lounge to the dining room. I really just wanted to kiss him and I knew he wouldn't have put up a fight. We didn't act out on it but I was later told that his girlfriend had heeded a warning that he should "stay away from that fucking woman!" so our mutual attraction may have been more conspicuous than we had thought.

Shortly after, I disappeared into my codependent heroin matrix and lost touch with Lloyd and everyone else who mattered. A few weeks after I married Robert, I got a Friend Request from Lloyd on Facebook. He was single and had moved to Joburg. He congratulated me on my blessed nuptials and we exchanged a few messages and then complete radio silence. Something inside of me broke a little and I couldn't explain this anomaly. Why was I mourning a man I hardly knew when I had just got married?

Trevor kept in contact over the next few months in what could only be described as a long-distance intervention. It involved a series of periodic telephonic exchanges between Trevor and me, as he updated me on Lloyd's status and level of denial, and I would instruct him on what to do next and how he should respond. Trevor was somewhat amazed that I could accurately predict his every move and counter-move.

"We're all the same," I assured him. "Predictable in our unpredictability."

One day he phoned to say that Lloyd had finally agreed to go to treatment. On his terms, of course.

"Take his house keys away," I instructed Trevor. "Make sure he has nowhere to go if he decides to leave rehab."

"Got it."

Trevor continued to phone with regular updates on how well Lloyd was doing at Houghton House, how well he looked and how different he appeared during visiting hours. I was even more elated when Trevor informed me that Lloyd had voluntarily agreed to extend his four-week mandatory stay to six weeks. It was working. It might have taken a year, but it was working.

The phone rang. Trevor's name flashed on my screen.

Oh fuck, I thought, something's happened.

"Hello," I answered, hiding my anxiety as best I could.

"Hi." It wasn't Trevor; it was Lloyd.

"Hey. How are you?"

"I'm good. I got out of 'Shady Pines' today. And I just wanted to call to say thank you."

I smiled broadly. I didn't know how much he knew of the role I had played in his intervention, but he clearly knew something. "You're welcome. Though I didn't do anything really."

"Some of the things T was saying this past year ..." he continued. "I knew those weren't his words. He told me you helped, a lot."

I laughed. "Yeah, he may have been channelling someone else."

"So, *ja*, thank you again."

"You're welcome. Stay in touch."

He did stay in touch. Almost every day for the next two months. We called each other, spending thousands of rand on airtime, talking into the early hours of the morning about everything and nothing and everything some more. I was suffering from severe insomnia so I relished our late-night conversations. He wasn't working yet, so I wasn't sure how he could afford the money for airtime.

"Don't you sleep?" he asked, one morning around 2 am.

"No," I said empathically. "And I don't cook either, just so you know." I had hardly been eating as a result of my new psych meds and loved the weight loss that came as a side effect.

"You realise," he said one night, "that the amount of money we're spending on airtime we could have bought airplane tickets and actually seen each other?"

"Then buy a ticket," I dared him. So he did, arriving on 30 November, barely three months sober, skinny, charming and missing two of his front teeth. But I didn't care. I was hooked. On him, on the idea of him, of us. I had smiled often to myself as I remembered the first time we met and how I knew, I just knew that we were going to be together one day. It was, of course to everyone else, a Terrible Idea. Farahnaaz issued the same warning: a Very Bad Idea. She took great pains to remind me of my past experience with a newcomer. But the day that he arrived from Joburg sealed our collective fate.

I picked Lloyd up from his sister's place and took him back to our flat where we spoke shyly, made out aggressively and then I fell asleep, my head on his chest. After weeks of insomnia, I passed out cuddled up to a man with whom I had just been reunited. Despite our long history, the truth was that I hardly knew him.

But I knew. I was finally safe.

CHAPTER 50

Conditional Love

I laid down three conditions if Lloyd wanted to be in a romantic relationship with me:

1. Move from Johannesburg to Cape Town.
2. Find gainful employment.
3. Get some new teeth.

I didn't think it was asking too much. I couldn't do long-distance relationships. I couldn't date a potential loser. Everyone needed to have their front teeth. Lloyd rose unexpectedly to the challenge but obtained employment and moved to the Mother City long before he got new teeth. He moved in with me and a very distrustful Isabella. She and I had been alone together, she woke up in my bed every morning (even though I put her to bed in her own every night). She was deeply unhappy that some strange toothless man had taken her place. Thankfully, Lloyd was very patient with her. He had no expectations of an instant bond, especially when Isabella's obvious jealousy made her attach to me almost surgically.

"Mommy, look at this!"

"Mommy, look at me!"

"Mommy, can we …?"

"Mommy, mommy, mommy!"

She called me by my parental title so frequently that I told her

I'd changed my name from Mommy to Patricia and she should only address me as such.

"Mommy, that's just stupid. Your name is Deathray-And-Martian," retorted my four-and-a-half-year-old.

It would take three long years before Bella vocally reciprocated Lloyd's love and affection for her. One night, in our new apartment in Kenilworth, I yelled out, "Goodnight, Belle. I love you."

"I love you too, Mommy," came the loud, affirmative responsive from her bedroom.

Lloyd gave it a go. "I love you, Belle."

Silence, then a quiet whisper travelled through the adjoining wall. "I love you too?" It was half self-questioning, half unsure, but the smile on Lloyd's face reassured both him and me that his patience had paid off. She loved him and she had said so.

I was adamant that I never wanted to get married again, and I told him so. I had also told him in no uncertain terms that I didn't want more children. I described in detail the horrors of pregnancy and my struggles with infants, in particular. He agreed. He had no children of his own and thought of Isabella as a daughter, so his family was complete.

Then suddenly, when Bella was eight, I decided that we should have a baby. I had no good reason. There was no void to be filled. My life was full enough. My practice was thriving, I loved spending time with Lloyd, Isabella was well adjusted despite being a product of a broken marriage. I had amazing, supportive, nurturing friendships. There was nothing missing. Being in a relationship with Lloyd had brought with it a sense of safety and security I hadn't imagined possible. He said he wasn't a cheater and I believed him – or at least really wanted to. He was kind and generous, the balm on my wounds. But somewhere deep inside I needed an emotional insurance policy of sorts. I thought that providing Lloyd with a child of his own would ensure that he stayed. I convinced him that there was no experience greater than having your *own* child despite my experiences to the contrary. And Isabella was such a great human being, our relationship was so loving and we were all so deeply connected.

I became obsessed – again. Multiple phone apps and ovulation tests (saliva and urine), pregnancy tests and fervent prayers to a God I didn't really trust followed. With every bloody, heavy period I got, I cried bitter tears of injustice and despondency. I eventually fell pregnant but the foetus was ectopic, lodged in my Fallopian tube instead of nestled in my uterus. I had to have surgery to have both the tube and the foetus removed and, upon awakening from the much-hated general anaesthetic and invasive procedure, promptly fell into a deep depression, repressing a cutting rage and inconsolable hurt that I hadn't felt in years.

Lloyd's proposal of marriage was neither romantic nor a huge fairy-tale gesture. He wasn't that kind of guy. For starters, there were no mountaintops or panoramic views. In fact, I was in bed one night when he knelt next to the bed beside me.

"What are you doing? Why the fuck are you acting so weird today?" I asked.

He showed me a ring, a ruby surrounded by diamonds and flanked by roses engraved in white gold.

"I want you to marry me." It wasn't a question.

I sat up. I was in my pyjamas and he was proposing marriage. It was incredibly surreal.

"Are you asking me?" I was already starting to cry.

"Yes."

"Then, yes."

That wedding saved me from myself. The detailed preparations – caterers, dress fittings, going to China Town to find decorations and jewellery – distracted me, drew me right out of the deep, dark depression that had descended and threatened to crush my psyche. It was three years to the day that he arrived in Cape Town and had the narcoleptic effect on me, that we married in a small ceremony in Camps Bay. We wrote our own vows and the marriage officer tacked the words "together forever" onto the end of my marital promises. I didn't believe in forever any more. But Lloyd knew that and was okay with it. My vows clearly stated "for a very long time". I was too polite to halt the wedding ceremony and correct him but Lloyd and I both laughed knowingly.

On our honeymoon, we discussed trying for a baby one more time. I would visit a fertility specialist and, if that didn't work, we'd call it quits. Lloyd couldn't tolerate seeing me in pain of any kind, but he also wanted to see an end to my neurotic fixation on conceiving. So I saw who was to become Scarlett before she was even conceived. The specialist did an internal ultrasound and pointed out the three eggs remaining in one ovary and the one that was about to "drop" during the next day or two. I looked at the monochrome slide on the doctor's fancy screen, at that one egg, and knew that that would become my baby. With Lloyd's input, of course.

"Go home and have lots of sex and keep your legs up," instructed Diana, who had accompanied me to the appointment. She was always there: at my divorce, at my hospital bed throughout all of the procedures, at my wedding and now. Since coming back into my life (which we maintained was the only reason Facebook had ever proven beneficial), she was steadfast in her ability to truly be there, wherever *there* happened to be.

I obediently followed instructions and eight much saner, medicated months later, Scarlett was born prematurely by emergency Caesarean, the umbilical cord wrapped twice around her neck, something that had not been detected on the ultrasound. With every contraction of my premature labour, it had tightened a little more, accelerating her heartbeat, increasing her distress. If they hadn't cut me open to get her out …

There was no music playing in the theatre that day, but there was a song dancing in my head as they once again scrubbed my insides and removed my second daughter.

It was 'My Girl' by The Temptations.

CHAPTER 51

Pills, Chills and Doctors' Bills

During my pregnancy I had gained 45 kilograms as a result of the meds that stopped me from cutting my own hair off or calling Lloyd a cunt. I was rotund and practically spherical. My feet had grown a whole shoe size. The baby, in comparison, was tiny at just 2.4 kilograms and had flawless white skin. Lloyd, although having all the outward appearances of being white, was in fact coloured – from Heideveld *nogal* – a fact that surprised a lot of people when they found out. So our collective ancestral gene pool produced a sweet-smelling, dark-haired newborn with alabaster skin. Once again, I'd be seen as the nanny or au pair – as I was when carting Isabella around as an infant.

The gargantuan weight gain, along with rampant post-partum hormones, caused that old familiar depression to creep back in. I was struggling with the infant, all her neediness and shameless vulnerability. But I had been right in my prediction that fatherhood would irrevocably change Lloyd. He was absolutely besotted with Scarlett and took to his new role with consummate, enviable ease. He did put the nappy on back to front his first time out, but that was an expected rookie mistake. He insisted on following my parenting lead and I kept asserting that I did not know the way.

Then Lloyd started a new job, which meant he had to travel frequently. I was not prepared for the radically destabilising effect it would have on me, left on my own with a helpless four-month-old child and precocious nine-year-old. On the simmering surface I was managing: they both got to school on time, they were fed and bathed, and I didn't beat them over the head with a breadboard. But I wept and mourned the loss of a husband who hadn't even left me. I went back to work – Scarlett went to daycare – but, after such a lengthy absence, I found it hard to attract new clients. As a result, I found my drive and motivation sliding into a cesspool of apathy and anger. I was angry with Lloyd for dismantling the sense of safety and security he had constructed around me, by travelling every week or two and being away for up to three weeks at a time. He was just working, but I felt utterly abandoned. I found my anger spilling out onto the children. I was deeply ashamed but told no one, not even Lloyd.

I changed psychiatrists after "Sleepy, The Dwarf" strongly suggested I stop breastfeeding at three months in favour of taking a mood stabiliser. He was clearly not sensitive to my status as a new mother, and I didn't want history to repeat itself. I wanted to engage in a pre-emptive strike against my encroaching depression. My new psychiatrist was well-respected, had seven framed certificates up on the wall and was a woman. She seemed genuinely sympathetic to my post-natal plight. She listened attentively to my long psychiatric history, mentioned that the weight gain could have been avoided with different medication, which just made me angrier with my previous shrink. Asshole. She then suggested a whole new course of medication: mood stabilisers, anxiolytics, antidepressants and sedatives. She said that my brain needed sleep in order to heal itself. I believed her – I wanted nothing more than to sleep – though I didn't trust the full-scale meds attack she was designing to combat my simmering symptoms. I was that one per cent of psych patients who always developed the rare side effect and here I was trying four new drugs at once. I was desperate not to slip into the abyss of chronic depression or rocket off into the stratospheric high of mania, so I complied by taking all the meds religiously. I ended up in a chemical straightjacket from which my brain quickly learned to escape.

It was 3.20 am. I only knew this because I had looked up at the gigantic clock mounted high up on the kitchen wall and made out the time through my blurred, cross-eyed vision, lurching forward drunkenly. I was in a definitive blackout state. I was almost sleepwalking, as though someone had slipped me that date rape drug psychopaths use on unsuspecting, vulnerable victims in bars. Only this was the result of prescribed medication meant to manage my current hypomanic episode. It was the third failed meds change in five days and the second blackout episode. During the first episode, which lasted about an hour and a half, I had done the strangest fucking things. I found myself 'waking up' in Isabella's room rifling through her drawers looking for God-knows-what. Later I'd come to in front of the bookshelf, unpacking books onto the floor and stacking them in piles. The previous night's episode was equally bizarre. I discovered that I had gone outside and taken down the damp laundry and left it in a pile on the garden chair. I also vaguely remembered preparing an imaginary meal and smoking unlit cigarettes. There was much repetitive opening and closing of cupboard and fridge doors. I eventually forced myself back to bed, to sleep, next to my two children, who were in our bed when Lloyd was away.

Oh my God, what if I tried to harm them? I cried myself to sleep.

I woke at 5.30 am and burst into desperate, frustrated tears for what had happened without my consent and for what may have gone so horribly wrong. I cried from extreme exhaustion and for the sheer strength it required to control my brain right now. I felt as though I was waiting for someone to take my hand and usher me like a madwoman into a clinic. My mind was overrun with dark, suicidal thoughts. I couldn't deal with my own bewildered brain, caught up in a perilous battle between the need to push through, to survive, to cope – as I'd always done – and just end it all. I needed help.

I phoned Lloyd.

"I need to go into a clinic."

"That bad?" He was genuinely concerned but I feared he wouldn't hear me.

"Yes." I paused. I needed to convey the seriousness of the situation. "I want to kill myself ... I'm scared for the children. You need to come home for two weeks so I can be admitted. Please."

He heard me. A few days later, after constant back-and-forth consultation with my therapist and psychiatrist, I was admitted to a private psychiatric hospital a few blocks from my home.

The counsellor was going back into treatment. What a monumental cluster-fuck.

I was not the perfect patient. I was everything I would've hated in a client: entitled, disengaged, apathetic, special and different. As we attempted to get the meds right again, I saw my psychiatrist every day. It was torturous trial-and-error and she encouraged me to not do much at all. I didn't need a second invitation.

I didn't want to see anyone. I didn't want to speak to the other patients. I just wanted to chain smoke and drink Energade in the covered courtyard in the back of the clinic and be left the fuck alone, me and my upside-down life. I didn't want to do fucking art therapy or fucking qi gong or talk about my feelings to these psychotic strangers. I only wanted to consult with my psychiatrist and my therapist who visited for a session once a week.

It was in one of these sessions that something shifted.

Georgia, my therapist, poured the rooibos tea, slowly, gracefully from the white issue teapot into the matching teacup without spilling a drop. I sucked and slurped noisily on the spout of my Energade bottle.

"I have hectic diarrhoea," I explained. "Everyone does."

Georgia nodded sympathetically and sipped her tea.

"How are you?" She was wearing her signature purple: a long, flowing floral skirt, lilac jersey, lavender shawl draped over her narrow shoulders and across her petite frame. Even her beanie was a hue of bruised grape, her long auburn hair falling like silk curtains from under the woolly hat. Diana and I called her 'The Fairy', for her uncanny knowledge of things mere mortals did not know, her hippy-ish otherworldly aura, as well her magical ability to piece back together the splintered parts of me. Session after session after session.

I was really broken this time, I thought, irreparably so.

"I'm fucking awful," I replied. I shifted my position in the upholstered wingback chair. I knew my discomfort was not about the chair. It was about wanting to end my life. There was nothing in the world that could placate these violent, vivid imaginings.

"Are you still feeling suicidal?" she asked in her gentle, soothing voice. Thunder began rumbling in the distance.

"Yes," I nodded.

The thunder was closer now, the weather as angry as my heart. Lightning cracked and crashed to the earth as I affirmed my desire to kill myself. Nature's external crisis was reflecting the emotional chaos lurching about in my heart and mind. It felt so beyond my control, this intolerable pain.

"Why do you want to punish everyone?" she asked, maintaining the soothing, dulcet tone, accompanied by a crash of well-timed lightning.

"What?" I asked, genuinely surprised by the question. I had become so self-involved in my own self-loathing that I had never thought of it in that light. But she was right. I didn't really want to die; I just wanted it all to stop. I wanted everyone to know how difficult it was: motherhood, working, being alone, having to pretend everything was okay all the time. Everything felt out of my control and my mind had unilaterally decided that suicide was the only option. It had not thought any further than that: the selfishness of such a gruesome act, hurting Lloyd beyond measure, leaving my children without a mother.

Georgia and I processed all of this, the weather providing an eerie, melodramatic soundtrack the entire hour. I knew then that if I didn't take responsibility for myself, my worst fear that Lloyd would leave me would come true: I would be left entirely alone. And so I committed to being emotionally honest with myself, and with him. I committed to taking care of the responsibilities I had chosen to take on to the best of my ability. The gory suicidal ideations lifted after about a week. The stripped-down meds regimen was taking. I was ready to go home, to what was really important: Lloyd, Isabella and Scarlett.

CHAPTER 52

Higher Learning

Scarlett was more interested in her dummy and her daddy than she was in my Big Day. Isabella had packed my teeny lunch into a Spiderman lunchbox given to me by Diana as a "back-to-school" gift. Excited and proud, Lloyd drove me there. I climbed out of the car and headed for the entrance to the Health Sciences campus of UCT. My tote bag, with *Queen of Fucking Everything* emblazoned in bold letters was filled with pretty notebooks and new stationery and hung strategically over my shoulder. I felt it too, proud and almost regal, as I swiped my student card at the turnstile at the entrance. I was a student at UCT. Finally. Only it was 20 years later.

I had undertaken the intensive process of applying for the Postgraduate Diploma in Addictions Care course and not only had I been accepted on Recognition of Prior Learning (my experience in the field of addictions counselling as apposed to any formal qualification), but also received a full bursary from the Department of Social Development.

I was 41 years old and returning to school. I was also 13 years sober. My private practice was flourishing and I had become a director/shareholder at Prospect Hill, which brought with it an unexpected sense of belonging. I was adulting hard.

I had a loving, supportive husband who was a great dad and worked his ass off to provide for us. I had two amazing daughters, each vastly different in personality. Isabella was gentle and sensitive and creative. Scarlett was wild, spirited and smart as a whip. I was a good mother – by no means perfect because I still threatened to sell them online from time to time. But I had moments of connection and tenderness with my daughters that had not been there before. I had worked tirelessly – with the help of my therapist as well as my sponsor, Zandri – through my family-of-origin issues and was able to parent my children in a way I had not been: with love, with boundaries, ensuring they felt emotionally and physically safe, ensuring that they felt heard.

I had also found my words again, those I had abandoned. I found them in the deep recesses of my mind, stored away in a Pandora's box, waiting to be released. They had waited patiently, my words, and when I was ready, I poured them out. My words were raw, honest and angry; they were bitter and brave and deeply sorrowful. But they were also hopeful. After silencing myself for decades, I was ready to be heard too, and I attended writing workshops and anxiously published short stories and poetry on a blog I created as well as in a poetry book that I self-published, purging years of unspoken pain, daring to speak about the things that we just never spoke about. I was blown away by the positive response. My words resonated with people. Yes, they proclaimed, I feel like that too! I felt profoundly connected to total strangers who affirmed that what I wrote, what I felt, was the truth. Not just mine but theirs too. I had survived to tell *our* story.

I had survived addiction, miscarriages, a retrenchment, job changes, multiple infidelities, an acrimonious divorce, single parenting, an ectopic pregnancy, raging manic highs and bleak, soul-destroying lows. I had survived postnatal depression (twice) and severe suicidality, madness and motherhood in recovery, multiple medication changes, the loss of important friendships to their relapses and just because it was time to let go of toxicity. I had made a formal arrangement with my messy brain that I would not fall carelessly into unmanageable lunacy again, that I would take care of myself and my delicate state of mind and not take my sanity for granted.

The last 13 years had been hard work – fucking hard. As I sat down to my first lecture as a postgraduate student, running my palm across the smooth, unblemished blank page of my notebook, I had one of those cheesy 'movie moments'. I would not be here if I hadn't stayed sober throughout each harrowing experience in recovery, if I hadn't asked for the help I needed when I needed it, if I hadn't surrounded myself with loving, functional relationships, if I hadn't done the difficult work on myself and unchained myself from my old, debilitating beliefs, if I hadn't loved myself back to a place of sanity. Life was gruelling. Sobriety was a two-faced bitch. But here I was, still standing.

I must have looked utterly foolish, grinning to myself in that lecture hall, but I didn't care. I had found my voice and the elusive love for which I had been so desperately searching my whole life. And it had been there the entire time, in the crowded basement of my own heart.

Acknowledgements

A book doesn't write itself; a life writes a book.

Many lives have penned this book, so thank you to my daughters, Isabella Rachael and Scarlett Grace, who are living, breathing, beautiful gifts of my unreal recovery. To my favourite husband, Lloyd, who allows me to spin like a whirlwind on my own axis until I am ready to face the world again (but doesn't do dishes).

To my Lead Lady Editor, Anna Szymonowicz, who often made my cluttered words make sense. To Sean Fraser, who treated those same words with such sensitivity and care.

To Bianca Lee, Hitomi, Samantha Constance, Alexa, Adam, Farahnaaz, Zandri and, my person, Nadine for their love, support and faith in me even when I had given up.

To Travers, who creates the music that expresses the words that most simply cannot and for showing me the meaning of family.

To Gillian, who is my safe place.

To the incomparable Dawn Garisch, who first told me that I was a writer. To the supremely talented Anastasya Eliseeva for my kick-ass cover. To Melinda Ferguson, my frighteningly divine publisher midwife, who told me to "go deeper" and "walk through those difficult doors", thank you for your belief in me.

To all of those who have helped me on this roller-coaster journey of recovery; you taught me how to speak my truth without fear or shame.

To my parents, who loved and supported me the best way they knew how.

And to all the hurt little – and grown-up – girls, this story is for you. There is always hope.

Always.